CHERIE FRESONKE

Clothed in

Righteousness

Adorned in the Fine Linen and
Breastplate of Righteousness

SUNFLOWER PRESS

Visit Sunflower Press online at www.sunflowerpress.net
Visit Cherie Fresonke's website at www.cheriefresonke.com

Clothed in Righteousness
Copyright © 2012 by Cherie Fresonke

Published by Sunflower Press
P.O. Box 813
Seal Beach, CA 90740
www.sunflowerpress.net

Cover Photograph taken by The Brothers Wright (BwrightPhoto.com).
Copyright by The Brothers Wright. All rights reserved.
Graphic design by Albena Tzvetkova
Edited by Mark Weising

ISBN: 978-0-9831678-7-7

Contents

By Way of Invitation

*H*ave you ever had a friend or relative who was walking down a path to destruction? Have you ever wondered why people make such wrong choices for their lives? These were just a few of the frustrating emotions I had as I was being jostled amongst the crowd on my way to an outdoor café to meet a young woman I had never met before. *She's walking down a path to destruction. Why is she making such wrong choices?*

The day before, the woman's aunt, in desperation, had come to see me. She told me that she was worried her niece was about to make the most devastating decision in her life. The young woman was considering leaving the country with a man she had just met. Given the nature of the region in which we were living, there was a high probability that if she left with this stranger, she would more than likely end up a victim of human trafficking.

As I pondered why I had offered this desperate aunt the invitation to have her niece speak to the "American woman" about her situation, my question to God was, "Lord, what could I possibly say to make a difference?"

It was then that I felt His still small voice impress these words on my heart: *Speak to her fear.*

When I arrived at the café and saw the young woman, my heart broke. She was so beautiful, and yet the emptiness she was feeling was causing her to make such poor choices. As her aunt began to share about the situation, God's whispered reminder—speak to her fear—emboldened me to ask, "Aren't you afraid you will be forced into prostitution and end up in a foreign country?"

The woman's aunt had asked her niece this same question just the day before. I remembered what the aunt had said was her niece's bold reply: "I would rather be a prostitute in a foreign country then live in the hopelessness this country has to offer." I was expecting the same answer this time. Instead, she offered a single whispered syllable: "Yes!"

It was then that this woman's aunt and I were able to help her realize that she needed to make wiser choices. Although it was a difficult process, she was ultimately able to break free from the clutches of this man who had so quickly entangled himself into her life.

When I walked away from the café that day, my heart was torn in two. I felt blessed that this young woman had chosen to break off the relationship, while at the same time I was broken to see how hopeless she felt. She was looking for love and acceptance in all the wrong places. She had bought into the lie that true fulfillment and contentment can be found just around the corner. She didn't understand the truth of who God was and the depths to which He loved her. She didn't realize that He desired her to come to Him, accept Him and learn from Him so she could walk in victory.

As I walked down those uneven cobblestone streets, God began to put this book on my heart. I rushed home and began to write. I knew that this young woman, and so many others like her, needed to know the truth about their identity in Christ. They needed to know that there is a battle—a spiritual battle—taking place all around them because of who God has called them to be. They needed to recognize the value of their lives so they could receive what God had created them to obtain.

Perhaps you have never found yourself in the same type of situation as this young woman. But have you ever looked for love in the wrong places? Have you ever run after one thing or another in an attempt to find true contentment and fulfillment? Have you ever felt as if you would never measure up? Have you ever thought that there is something missing that you can't quite grasp? Have you ever felt empty or hopeless?

I have been discipling brokenhearted people since 1993 in both the United States and Eastern Europe. During the many years that God has used me in ministry, I have discovered two important aspects of the Christian life that we often don't fully understand or apply to our lives. The first is that we have been given a *new identity in Christ* that has the power to set us free from the bondage of sin. The second is that we have an *enemy of our souls* who desires to destroy us. If we don't have a balanced, biblical understanding of who he is and how he operates, we will never walk in victory. When we understand these two aspects and apply the truth that God reveals to us about them, we can begin to live up to our true calling.

As you read this book, you will discover that I have written each chapter as if I were a character commissioned by the King of kings to write to *you* personally. These letters explain the truth about the King of kings, who loves you deeply; His Son, the Prince of Peace, who came to save you; The Royal Counselor, who is with you always; and Lucifer, the archenemy, who seeks ways to wreak havoc in your life. The letters were written in love so you can begin to resist the enemy's schemes and grow in your relationship with God.

Each letter will also encourage you to move the truth you discover of who you are in Christ from your *head* to your *heart*. Although most believers know they are loved, forgiven and set free from sin on an intellectual level, they do not believe these truths *deep within their hearts*. They do not apply these principles to their lives, which gives Satan a stronghold to keep them bound in defeat. Because they do not have a biblical understanding of who Satan is and how he operates, they remain entangled in their sin and stagnant in their relationship with the Lord.

No matter where you are in your walk with God, there are golden nuggets to be discovered in each letter. While the letters are arranged in sequential order—from curiosity about the things of God to deeper spiritual truths about victorious living—don't skip ahead. Each letter will reveal different aspects about your identity in Christ and, more importantly, show you ways to apply this truth so you will have true meaning and fulfillment. For this reason, no matter where you are in your walk with God, be open to what He wants to do in your heart and mind—and know that every truth contained within is based on God's Word.

If you have ever struggled with knowing who you are, or you desire to find true peace and contentment, or you want to stop making decisions based on feelings and emotions, I invite you to turn the pages. The King of kings wants you to discover the truth of who you are and why He gave you life! He will speak to you and show you how much you are worth if you are willing to open your heart to Him and hear what He has to say. He loves you more than you will ever know.

Note: Make sure to purchase and complete the companion Bible study to this book so you can see the truth of God's Word for yourself. It is excellent for personal study or use in weekly Bible study groups. (See page 223.)

Chapter One

Clothed in Love

You Are Loved

The LORD appeared to us in the past, saying:
"I have loved you with an everlasting love;
I have drawn you with loving-kindness."
Jeremiah 31:3

*D*ear Precious Friend,

I'm writing to tell you about some amazing truths that up until now may have been concealed from you. It's about the King of kings and how much He loves you. In fact, He loves you so much that He commissioned me to write a series of letters to you to explain why you were given life. The King has been preparing your heart to receive this information, and my prayer is that you will wait expectantly for these letters and ponder the words you find within. For it is in this pondering that a deep heart-work will begin.

Now, you may not immediately accept my claim that there *is* a King. Whether or not you believe this is true does not matter at the moment—this letter was not written to convince you of that fact. Instead, it is to prepare you for the battle that is soon to come. Some of your greatest triumphs and deepest struggles lie directly ahead.

Although you may not realize it—or even possibly accept it—there *is* a fierce battle surrounding you because of

5

who you are called to be. On the one side is the King, who loves you and has called you to serve with Him. On the other side is the enemy of your soul—yes, you *do* have an enemy—who is determined to keep you from joining with the King. Any time the King's throne is involved, there is going to be warfare.

You may ask, "Who is this enemy?" His name is Lucifer, and he was originally one of the King's servants. But he was proud and desired the King's throne, so he was commanded to leave the Kingdom. When Lucifer left, he took a third of the King's knights with him, and there has been a tremendous battle raging ever since. Unfortunately, this battle includes *you*. It is a battle over whom you will choose to be aligned . . . a battle for your very soul. This is why you must be prepared. Although this battle is spiritual and is fought in the heavenly realms—which is why you can't see it—you will either benefit or suffer from the outcome.

Let me explain some of the enemy's tactics and the methods he uses to continually wage this battle against you. First, Lucifer comes up with a lie that he hopes to use to deceive you. Second, he gets the world to sell the lie by enticing you to believe that it is true. Third, he tempts your flesh to buy the lie. When you give in to this temptation, he has succeeded in his plan. It is these three influences that cause the daily inward struggle in your life.

Here's an example of how this works. Let's say that Lucifer wants you to believe that to be a person of status, you must be rich and beautiful, accepted by others, and achieve certain accomplishments. He gets the world to sell this deception by constantly bombarding you with advertising and claims that build this façade. When your flesh accepts this lie, he can keep you constantly running around, desiring to be someone you are not, never truly finding fulfillment.

Can you remember a time in your life when you saw this play out? Maybe you bought into the lie that you weren't as pretty or handsome as those around you. Or you were deceived into believing you were an outsider and didn't quite fit in with the crowd. Or maybe Lucifer has duped you into believing that you had to achieve one thing or another to feel good about yourself. We want to be loved and accepted by those around us, and the enemy will use this to his advantage.

I know how this works because when I was young, I, myself, desired so deeply to be accepted that I tried to find love in all the wrong places. Although my story is different from yours, the enemy used these same tactics to keep me on the wrong path. The choices I made for my life—all out of the desire to fit in and be loved and accepted—led me down the road to destruction.

Lucifer, the schemer, would like nothing better than to keep you and me in this vicious cycle of life. He knows that if he can keep us in this pattern of defeat, we will deny who the King desires us to be. If he can keep us running in circles trying to find fulfillment everywhere, we will ultimately find it nowhere, and we will never achieve all that the King created us to be.

But there is truth—and that truth will set us free. The King of kings led me to discover this truth, which is why He has commissioned me to share this truth with you. He wants you to know that there *is* a better way. In fact, it is the most wonderful way of all!

Now, perhaps you are thinking, *I'm not that special. Why would the King commission someone to write to a person like me?* That is part of the enemy's strategy—his warfare. Lucifer, the deceiver, has whispered this lie into your ear. The world has sold this lie with its relentless advertising campaigns. It has convinced you that you need this or that to be special—and then has led you to believe that you are *not* that special because you can't possess all those things—no matter what those things or relationships are. When this happens, your flesh has bought the lie.

The truth is that you *are* someone special simply because the King *says* you are special. If you can accept and embrace this truth, you will walk—not stumble, but walk—victoriously through life, for you will have the ability to be more than a conqueror. You will come to know why you were given life. You will come to realize that the King loves you so deeply that He desires to have a real, personal, intimate relationship with you. You will come to know His perfect will for your life. And you will come to understand that it is because of Him that you can be clothed in righteousness. Until that time, just know that you are clothed in love.

You see, there is a reason—a wonderful reason—why you were given life! Your life has true meaning, value and purpose. Lucifer knows this is the truth, which is why he will do anything within his power to keep you from embracing it. This is why I have written this letter—I want to pass on to you this legacy of knowing who the King desires you to be. I want you to come to accept the treasure of the depth of the love the King has for you that surpasses all knowledge so you can triumph over all of the enemy's schemes.

Please know, my dear precious friend, that I am praying for you. Soon I will find a way to get my next letter to you—the letter in which I will begin to teach you about the secret place where precious treasures are to be stored and cherished. Until then, let the truth of the King's Word and His love for you begin to penetrate deep into your heart. Let Him hear you say it: *"I am loved."*

And, though you may not yet believe it, I challenge you to whisper, *"I am someone special."* I encourage you to ponder this truth in the depth of your heart.

Always remember that the King is drawing you to Himself with His lovingkindness. So go ahead and declare it one more time: *"I am loved!"*

Until the time I can write to you again, always remember that I hold you dear to my heart.

In awe of His love,
Your Willing Servant of the King

Chapter Two

Woven Together

You Are Not a Mistake

*You made all the delicate, inner parts of my body
and knit me together in my mother's womb.
Thank you for making me so wonderfully complex!
Your workmanship is marvelous—how well I know it.*
Psalm 139:13-14, NLT

*D*ear Precious Friend,

Have you ever been discontent, yearning for something
that you can't quite describe? Have you ever pondered why
you are not fully satisfied? Well, in my first letter, I promised that I would write about the secret place where precious
treasures are stored and cherished—which holds the key to
these questions. Before you discover this secret place, however, I want you to know about the King of kings and His
Son, the Prince of Peace, who desires to bring His perfect
peace to your life. Although you may not know it, you are
special to the King and His Son. In fact, it was His hands in
love that formed you at the moment of your conception.

Your Creator, the King, is the one and only ruler of the
universe, and He holds your very breath in His hands. He
created the heavens and the earth, and He created you in
His own image and likeness. This simply means that He
patterned and fashioned you after Himself.[1] This is what

sets you apart and places you above the fish of the sea, the birds of the air, the livestock of the fields, and over the entire earth.

Nothing the King created happened by chance. The idea that everything evolved randomly over time is a lie that Lucifer, the deceiver, would like you to believe. He wants you to think you are only an accident of nature—a mere mistake. If you choose to believe this lie, then it will be easier for the betrayer to convince you that you are not unique nor uniquely created. This is not the truth! Your Creator, the King, fashioned you in wisdom with a specific purpose in mind.

Throughout history, many great thinkers have asked, "What is man?" Philosophers, scientists, psychologists and anthropologists have all explored this topic, and they have struggled in coming up with a plausible answer. Eventually, the only conclusion that can be reached is that man is *wonderfully made.*

David, the King's own psalmist and one of His greatest scribes, once asked, "What is man that you are mindful of him, the son of man that you care for him?" (Psalm 8:4). The King inspired many such wonderful scribes—40, to be exact—and they have written a collection of 66 books (known as the Word) that tells of your heritage. Many times I will quote from this Book, for it is foundational to what you are learning and will tell about the struggles you will encounter in life. In one of these books known as Psalms, David, speaking of the Creator, your King, writes:

> You made all the delicate, inner parts of my body and knit me together in my mother's womb. Thank you for making me so wonderfully complex! Your workmanship is marvelous—and how well I know it. You watched me as I was being formed in utter seclusion,

as I was woven together in the dark of the womb. You
saw me before I was born. Every day of my life was
recorded in your book. Every moment was laid out
before a single day had passed.
—Psalm 139:13-16, NLT

As this passage states, you were woven together by your
Creator, the King. However, Lucifer, the liar, would like to
convince you that this is not the truth. After all, we all know
a man and a woman can decide to have a child, and it seems
as if *they* created it. But the King plays the *most important*
role in how each child is fashioned together in its mother's
womb. Every child is unique and precious to Him, and from
the moment of conception He is there, watching and working as the baby is formed in utter seclusion.

At the moment of conception, each new life inherits 23
chromosomes from its parents, for a total of 46 in all. From
this point, the cell (called an embryo) begins to divide at a
tremendous rate. One cell becomes two, then two become
four, and then four become eight. At some point, early in
this growth, the cells begin to specialize. Some become the
respiratory system, some the skeletal system, some the ner-
vous system, and so on. To this day, medical science cannot explain how the cells *know* to begin to differentiate, but
there is someone who does:

As you do not know the path of the wind, or how the
body is formed in a mother's womb, so you cannot
understand the work of God, the Maker of all things.
—Ecclesiastes 11:5

My precious friend, it is the King who knit and wove
you together. You are a work of art and not a mistake—no
matter what others may say! Although your mother, your
father, your sister and your brother may forget you, the

King will never do so. Look at another wonderful truth contained within the Word:

> Can a mother forget the baby at her breast and have no compassion on the child she has borne? Though she may forget, I will not forget you! See, I have engraved you on the palms of my hands.
>
> —Isaiah 49:15-16

The King loves you so much that He promises to *never* forget you. He has engraved you on the palms of His hands. In fact, you are always in His thoughts.

When your Creator, the King, formed the first man, He breathed life into him, and man became a living soul. He created humans in His image and likeness to enable them to make their own choices—to be able to think, analyze and reflect on abstract matters. In this way, humans became uniquely different from the animals, for the King intended humans to be both physically *and* spiritually alive. The reason the King created humans in this manner is because of His deep love for them. Even more amazing He desires to have a real, personal, intimate relationship with *you*.

Because Lucifer is also known as the author of confusion, it is important to define the word "intimate." If you were to look in a thesaurus, you would find the following synonyms: "familiar," "close," "dear," "personal," "confidential," "private," "trusted," "secret," "deep" and "detailed." These words describe the intimate relationship the King desires to have with you—yes, you! He wants to be your friend, your confidant, your advocate, your supporter, your provider, your sympathizer and your companion. He desires to be your best friend—the lover of your soul.

Now, as I promised, I want to tell you about the "secret place." It is interesting to note that there are two other words associated with the word "intimate": "inner" and "inmost."

Your Creator, the King, developed your *inmost* being—a secret place in the depths of your heart—where precious treasures are to be stored and cherished. He put a deep yearning for love within you—a yearning for a *divine* love that can only be filled through a right relationship with Him. Listen to what the psalmist wrote:

> My soul longs, yes, faints for the courts of the LORD;
> my heart and flesh sing for joy to the living God.
> —Psalm 84:2, ESV

> O God, you are my God; earnestly I seek you; my soul thirsts for you; my flesh faints for you, as in a dry and weary land where there is no water.
> —Psalm 63:1, ESV

The King created you with this yearning for a divine and intimate relationship with Him. However, Lucifer will do everything in his power to try to prevent this from happening. He will lie to you and try to get you to fill this yearning in ways that are unpleasing to the King, such as through wrong relationships with others, material possessions, career ambitions, knowledge, fame, drugs, alcohol and so forth. Lucifer will even try to confuse you with religion and tradition. Remember that by trying to find fulfillment everywhere, you will find it nowhere. The only way you will be able to satisfy the deep yearning that the King has placed inside of you is through a right relationship with Him.

I believe the King created a hole in the depths of your heart that can only be filled through a right relationship with Him. This is the secret place He specifically created for you to meet in intimate fellowship with Him so that precious treasures can be stored and cherished there deep within your heart. He wants to build an intimate relationship by meeting with you in your innermost being each day.

15

So continue to read my letters, for they will explain in more detail how you can develop this real, personal, intimate relationship and find true fulfillment in the secret place in the depths of your own heart.

With all this said, never forget that the King created you in His own image. Let Him hear you state it: *"I am created in the King's image."*

You have been wonderfully made for a specific purpose. Whisper it in awe: *"I am wonderfully made."*

You were not a mistake, no matter what others may have said to the contrary. Understand it and accept it: *"I am not a mistake."*

The King, out of His deep love for you, created you with an inmost being—a secret place—in the depths of your heart. Ponder the King's love as you quote it: *"I am created with an inmost being."*

You have been created in this manner so that you would desire to have an intimate relationship with the King. Let Him hear you embrace it: *"I am created with a yearning desire to have an intimate relationship with the King of kings."*

Cherish these truths that the King has written deep within your heart. In the meantime, I pray that you will look with hope for my next letter, because in it I will give you a much deeper understanding of the struggle that surrounds you. Until then, may the King protect you.

Woven together for this divine assignment of love,
Your Faithful Servant of the King

Chapter Three

Wrapped in the Cord of Sin

You Are Free to Choose

*"What is man, that he could be pure,
or one born of woman, that he could be righteous?"*
Job 15:14

$\mathcal{D}$ear Precious Friend,

Are you beginning to grasp the deep love the King has for you? Can you feel His lovingkindness drawing you closer? Now that you understand you were created in the King's own image and woven together in your mother's womb, you are prepared to learn more about who you are and why there is such a fierce battle surrounding you.

It is the King's desire that you come to a place where you realize your life has true meaning and that you understand the specific purpose for which you were created. So, to bring you to that place, let's read some verses found in the Word. Ezekiel, another of the King's scribes, penned these verses that are found in the book named after him:

> On the day you were born your cord was not cut, nor were you washed with water to make you clean, nor were you rubbed with salt or wrapped in cloths. No one looked on you with pity or had compassion enough to do any of these things for you. Rather, you

were thrown out into the open field, for on the day you were born you were despised.

Then I passed by and saw you kicking about in your blood, and as you lay there in your blood I said to you, "Live!" I made you grow like a plant of the field. You grew up and developed and became the most beautiful of jewels. Your breasts were formed and your hair grew, you who were naked and bare.

Later I passed by, and when I looked at you and saw that you were old enough for love, I spread the corner of my garment over you and covered your nakedness. I gave you my solemn oath and entered into a covenant with you, declares the Sovereign LORD, and you became mine.

I bathed you with water and washed the blood from you and put ointments on you. I clothed you with an embroidered dress and put leather sandals on you. I dressed you in fine linen and covered you with costly garments. I adorned you with jewelry: I put bracelets on your arms and a necklace around your neck, and I put a ring on your nose, earrings on your ears and a beautiful crown on your head. So you were adorned with gold and silver; your clothes were of fine linen and costly fabric and embroidered cloth. Your food was fine flour, honey and olive oil. You became very beautiful and rose to be a queen. And your fame spread among the nations on account of your beauty, because the splendor I had given you made your beauty perfect, declares the Sovereign LORD.

—Ezekiel 16:4-14

Ezekiel wrote these verses specifically to the nation of Israel, but they apply to your life as well. Note the scribe's words near the beginning of this passage: "On the day you were born your cord was not cut." This describes why you struggle as you do. Allow me to explain.

In my previous letter, I told you that your Creator, the King, breathed life into the first man and made him in His image. This man, Adam, and his wife, Eve, are distant relatives of yours. Even though you were *created* in the image and likeness of the King, you were *born* in the image and likeness of Adam and Eve. Unfortunately, this means that you inherited certain things from them—including a grave disease they contracted as a result of a choice they made. This disease is actually the "cord" of which Ezekiel writes. It is a cord of sin and death that has kept all of Adam and Eve's descendants shackled and in slavery since the beginning of time.

It all began back in a garden known as Eden. After the King created Adam and his wife, Eve, He placed them in this garden and abundantly provided for all of their needs. The King gave them only one restriction. As we read in the Word, He said to Adam, "You are free to eat from any tree in the garden; but you must not eat from the tree of the knowledge of good and evil, for when you eat of it you will surely die" (Genesis 2:16-17). It was at this point in history that Lucifer, the former servant of the King who had been cast down to earth because of his pride, intertwined himself in the story.

One day, he found Eve in the Garden. He approached her in the form of a serpent and asked, "Did [the King] really say, 'You must not eat from any tree in the garden'?" (Genesis 3:1b). Lucifer, though he chose to become a traitor, is extremely smart and knows the Word remarkably well, and one of his common tricks is to try to twist it to cause confusion. Eve, unaware of the dangerous ground on which she was treading, explained the decree of the King: "We may eat fruit from the trees in the garden, but God did say, 'You must not eat fruit from the tree that is in the middle of the garden, and you must not touch it, or you will die'" (Genesis 3:2b-3).

In fact, the King never told Adam and Eve that they could not *touch* the tree. Peter, another scribe of the King, would later write that Lucifer is like "a roaring lion looking for someone to devour" (1 Peter 5:8), and Eve's lack of knowledge of the King's Word might have served as the opening he needed to pounce. Note how Lucifer was able to twist the King's words just enough to cause Eve to doubt: "You will not surely die. . . . For [the King] knows that when you eat of it your eyes will be opened, and you will be like [Him], knowing good and evil" (Genesis 3:4-5).

Remember the three tactics I described in a previous letter on how the enemy deceives people? These three tactics have not changed in thousands of years; in fact, they are the same three tactics he used against Adam and Eve. First, Lucifer thought up a lie: Adam and Eve would *not* die if they ate from the forbidden tree. Next, Lucifer cleverly used the beauty of Eve's world system to weave his web of deceit for future generations: "The woman saw that the fruit of the tree was good for food and pleasing to the eye" (Genesis 3:6a). Eve believed the lie of the traitor and fell to her own fleshly desires, which led to this devastating result:

> When the woman saw that the fruit of the tree was good for food and pleasing to the eye, and also desirable for gaining wisdom, she took some and ate it. She also gave some to her husband, who was with her, and he ate it.
>
> —Genesis 3:6

As this story shows, you must always be on the alert for Lucifer's deceptions, for when he lies he speaks his native tongue (see John 8:44). You cannot lower your defenses for even a moment, because it is just too easy to fall into one of

Lucifer's well-woven traps. In a future letter I will train you in using the weapons the King has provided to combat the enemy, but for now I want you to be aware of his tricks. One of the best ways to learn how to overcome your adversary is to learn from your mistakes and the mistakes of others—in this case, the mistakes of Adam and Eve.

There is another important aspect of this account that cannot be overlooked: Adam, Eve's husband, was with her when she was deceived. The King had placed him over Eve, and it was his duty to protect her, but he also followed his fleshly desires. He allowed Eve to eat the forbidden fruit, and then joined her. He fell short of the duties the King had assigned to him, and because of his disobedience, human-kind has been plagued with a terrible disease—a disease of sin that results in death. What the King had warned against had come to pass: "You must not eat from the tree of the knowledge of good and evil, for when you eat of it you will surely die" (Genesis 2:17).

Yes, it is true that you have inherited this deadly disease. As the King's scribe Paul once wrote:

> When Adam sinned, sin entered the world. Adam's sin brought death, so death spread to everyone, for every-one sinned.
>
> —Romans 5:12, NLT

You were born *physically alive*, but *spiritually dead*. You were "thrown out into the open field," as Ezekiel wrote. You did not have the King's presence in your life or the knowl-edge of His ways. Job, a man who once suffered great loss at the hands of Lucifer, once asked the King, "What is man, that he could be pure, or one born of woman, that he could be righteous?" (Job 15:14). Job understood that all humans had inherited this deadly disease from Adam and Eve. The cord tying you to Adam and Eve was not cut, nor were you "wrapped in cloth," because you were born unrighteous. Although the King wove and knit you together in your mother's womb, you were sinful from the moment of conception. As David, the King's psalmist, wrote, "Surely I was sinful at birth, sinful from the time my mother conceived me" (Psalm 51:5).

Have you ever pondered the fact that while you desire to do good, you cannot achieve it? Paul commented on this when he wrote, "I want to do what is good, but I don't. I don't want to do what is wrong, but I do it anyway" (Romans 7:19, NLT). Because of Adam and Eve's disobedience in the Garden, you were born under the power and authority of Lucifer, the god of this age, which has caused you to be shackled and chained as a slave to sin.

Furthermore, you were born to suffer not only spiritual death but also physical death. The relationship with your Creator was severed in the Garden, and unless you choose to realign yourself with the King, you will forever suffer separation from Him. For after you die physically, you will be thrown into a dungeon known as the lake of fire. As the King's Word declares:

> If anyone's name [is] not found written in the book of
> life, he [will be] thrown into the lake of fire.
> —Revelation 20:15

Let me sum it up for you: Because of Adam and Eve's fall, you were *born* in the image and likeness of Adam rather than the King. You were *born* with sin present in your physical body. You were *born* with a spirit that is dead to the King. You were *born* under the power and authority of Lucifer. You were *born* a slave to sin. You were *born* to suffer physical death. And you were *born* with the lake of fire as your eternal destination.[1]

But there is good news—in fact, the most wonderful news in all of history! Even though you were clothed in sin at birth, you can choose to be clothed in righteousness now. One of the King's names in Hebrew is Jehovah-Rapha, which means "the Lord Our Healer." He is the Great Physician, and He has provided a cure—a most wonderful cure—to redeem you from this life of sin and death! So take heart, my dear precious friend, and remember the love the King has for you. It is a love so deep that He risked all to give you a choice—the choice of love.

The King has made a way to rescue you from this life of destruction, and it is all found within a gift—an incredible gift. But it is up to you as to whether you will accept it. Just as Adam and Eve were given the choice to accept God's gift of life or believe the deceiver and accept death, you have a choice before you today. So consider the wonder of this appeal and repeat it out loud: *"I am free to choose."*

It is my prayer that you will take this letter to heart and ponder these truths deep within the secret place—for your very life depends on it. Remember that in the heavenly realm there is a fierce battle being waged for your eternal soul. Lucifer does not want you to choose to accept the King's gift, and he will use all of the tactics at his disposal to keep you wrapped in the cords of sin.

In the meantime, wait for my next letter with eager anticipation, for within it I will describe the gift of hope that awaits you—the cure that will heal you. Until then, may the royal army of the King protect you.

Serving the King in love,
Your Willing Servant

Chapter Four

Clothed in
Garments of Salvation

You Are Saved

But God demonstrates his own love for us in this:
While we were still sinners, Christ died for us.
Romans 5:8

$\mathcal{D}$ear Precious Friend,

In my previous letter, I promised I would write to you about the wonderful gift that awaits you. It is a gift full of precious treasures that only the King can bestow. The value of this gift is immeasurable, because it will not only fill your emptiness inside but also give you riches that will last for eternity.

Since we have never met, I must assume that you do not know about this gift. However, even if you do—and even if you have already received it—please don't stop reading this letter, for I am going to share some precious truths with you that you can cherish deep within the secret place in the depth of your heart. Furthermore, Lucifer would like nothing better than to diminish the importance of this gift—or convince you that you don't really need it—so I want to explain everything about it to you.

As I have previously written, the King of kings is not like any earthly king. He operates outside of *space and time,* so He can actually see your life as if it had already passed. He ordained *every day that you will experience* even before you were born, and He has written all the days you will ever have in His Book of Life. The King has always been and forever will be. In other words, He is *eternal.* Even more, He has the ability (and the desire) to make you a citizen of the Kingdom and grant you an eternity with Him as a member of His own family.

Before I tell you more, there is an important question I want you to ponder deep within your heart. This question is so important that you must answer it with absolute honesty. Ponder this: *If you were to die today, where would you spend eternity?* Do you know without a doubt that you are a citizen of the Kingdom, or has the deceiver led you to believe that you can refuse to accept this gift and still have eternal life? This is a critical question, because the King will never force His gift on anyone. In order to receive it, *you* must personally make the choice as to whom you will serve.

In my last letter, I told you that you were born into this world under the power and authority of Lucifer, the traitor. This means that unless you choose to accept the King's gift and align yourself with His side, you will not receive any of the privileges of being His child. Many people falsely believe that because they were born into a country that considers itself part of the Kingdom, they are automatically children of the King. Or they believe that because their mother or father was a citizen of the Kingdom, they also have attained this status. Or they believe they are children of the King because they go to His house to pray, or are such "good people" that they are automatically given citizenship. I am sorry to tell you that these are just lies of Lucifer, the father of lies.

In fact, if you decide *not* to align yourself with the King, you arbitrarily align yourself with Lucifer, for you are either with the King or against the King. There is no middle ground. As I told you, "on the day you were born you were despised" (Ezekiel 16:5). Lucifer, the murderer, *despised* you and not only wanted you to die *physically* but also wanted you to remain *spiritually* dead. On the day you were born, the cord of sin and death—the cord that ties you to Adam—was not cut. You were born shackled and in slavery to sin. But the King made a way for this cord to be severed so you could be set free from sin and death. This wonderful way is found within the gift.

As Paul writes, "[The King] demonstrates his own love for us in this: While we were still sinners, [the Prince of Peace] died for us" (Romans 5:8). John, another of the King's scribes, explains it this way: "For [the King] so loved the world that he gave his one and only Son, that whoever believes in him shall not perish but have eternal life" (John 3:16). Because of the King's deep love for you, He sent His one and only Son—the Prince of Peace—to *die* so you may have eternal life. It was the only way to cut the cord and save you from the eternal destruction that awaited you.

At this point, you might be wondering how the King was able to send His own Son into the world and bring about this incredible defeat against the enemy. To explain, I will once again refer to the King's Word, which tells the story how the Prince of Peace entered the earth and the works He performed there. His conception is one of my favorite stories told in the Book, and since my writing cannot compare to the beauty of the Word, I will simply quote this miraculous event.

> [The King] sent the angel Gabriel to Nazareth, a town in Galilee, to a virgin pledged to be married to a man named Joseph, a descendent of David.

The virgin's name was Mary. The angel went to her and said, "Greetings, you who are highly favored! The Lord is with you."

Mary was greatly troubled at his words and wondered what kind of greeting this might be. But the angel said to her, "Do not be afraid, Mary, you have found favor with [the King]. You will be with child and give birth to a son, and you are to give him the name Jesus [the Prince of Peace]. He will be great and will be called the Son of the Most High. . . . His kingdom will never end."

"How will this be," Mary asked the angel, "since I am a virgin?"

The angel answered, "The Holy Spirit will come upon you, and the power of the Most High will overshadow you. So the holy one to be born will be called the Son of [the King]."

—Luke 1:26-35

The Prince's conception and birth are significant, for they explain how He could be both fully man (born of a virgin, Mary) and yet fully the King's Son (born without sin). In fact, the Prince of Peace was *not* born in the image and likeness of Adam, nor was He from the line of Adam. Therefore, "just as through the disobedience of the one man [Adam] the many were made sinners, so also through the obedience of the one man [the King's Son] the many will be made righteous" (Romans 5:19).

Notice in the above passage what the angel says to Mary: "You will be with child and give birth to a son, and you are to give him the name Jesus" (Luke 1:31). The King's Son has many names besides the Prince of Peace, and many know Him by this name: Jesus Christ. In Matthew 1:21 found in the Word, an angel said to Joseph, Mary's future husband, that he was to give the child "the name Jesus, because he will save his people from their sins." The name "Jesus" literally means "the Lord saves,"[1] while the name "Christ" means "the Anointed One."[2] Therefore, "Jesus Christ" is the Anointed One who saves.

Although it is difficult to fathom, the Prince of Peace has been with the King from the beginning of time, and He and the King are one. As John writes, "In the beginning was the Word [referring to the Prince of Peace, for this is another of His names], and the Word was with God [the King], and the Word was God [for the King and His Son are one]. He was with God [the King] in the beginning. Through him [again speaking of the Prince of Peace] all things were made" (John 1:1-3). In fact, the King of kings is evident in three distinct persons: the King (also known as God the Father), the Son (Jesus Christ, the Prince of Peace), and the Royal Counselor (the Holy Spirit).

As I've stated, the King loved you so deeply that He sacrificed His Son, the Prince of Peace, so you could have eternal life. The Prince of Peace, in turn, loved you so deeply that He *willingly* gave up His life to save yours. But it didn't just end there. Three days after the Prince's sacrifice of love, He physically rose from the grave. "Physically" means that He literally, in bodily form, came back to life. Death could not hold him! Paul tells us in 1 Corinthians 15:6 that He appeared to more than 500 eyewitnesses, after which He ascended to heaven and sat down at the right hand of the King, where He lives today.

So, now you know why the King sent His Son into the world and how the Prince of Peace was able to conquer death and free you from your sins. You also know that through the sacrifice of the Prince of Peace, you have been given the ability to accept the gift of eternal life. But maybe you are still not convinced that you are in need of the King's salvation.

Maybe you are still stuck in the mindset that you are a "good person" and that you haven't done anything "bad enough" to keep you from eternal life. Let's return again to the King's Word to see exactly what it says about your condition.

Once again, Paul sums it up well: "For all have sinned and fall short of the glory of God" (Romans 3:23). Notice the word "all." *Everyone* has sinned and fallen short of the King's glory. This means that there is not one person in the course of human history who has been without sin, except for the King's Son, the Prince of Peace, Jesus Christ. But what is sin? In the original language, the word "sin" literally means "to miss the mark."[3] This raises another question: miss the mark of what?

You are probably aware of the Ten Commandments, but did you know that before the Prince of Peace came into the world, there were actually 613 different decrees the King required to be kept?[4] This was known as the Law, and it was the King's measure of righteousness. Those who could not meet the Law—because of wrong actions, wrong attitudes *or* wrong thoughts—were guilty of committing sin. In other words, they were guilty of missing the mark the King had set.

In fact, no one was ever able to measure up to the King's standard, which once again proves that everyone is born into sin. However, there was a blessing contained within the Law, for it was given to point people to the King's Son, the Prince of Peace, who alone could free them from the penalty of sin. As I have mentioned, this penalty is *death* (see Romans 6:23)—and not just a *physical* death but also a *spiritual* death, which includes an *eternal* separation from the King of kings. The truth is that each person will spend eternity in one of two places: with the King or without Him. No one is exempt. Whether you believe this to be true or not does not matter—it is a fact simply because the King says it is so. Nonetheless, the most wonderful news of all is that "the gift of God is eternal life in Christ Jesus our Lord" (Romans 6:23b). This is the gift I've been writing to you about—the most wonderful gift of all.

Now, if you have been closely following what I have been saying up to this point, a few questions might be forming in your mind: *If the King is eternal and all-powerful, why did He have to send His Son to die for our sins? Couldn't He just wave them away or speak them out of existence?* The reason a sacrifice was needed is because the King is holy and cannot look upon sin. Sin separated Him from His creation, and the only way that relationship could be restored was for those sins to be "covered over" and washed clean by the blood of the Lamb. (By the way, this is another name for the Prince of Peace—the Lamb of God.)

When Adam and Eve sinned in the Garden of Eden, they could no longer stand rightly before the King because of the shame of their sin. Therefore, "they sewed fig leaves together and made coverings for themselves" (Genesis 3:7b). But this was not a sufficient covering, so they hid from the King. The same is true for us today; because of our sin, we are unable to stand in the presence of the King. In order to restore the relationship, there must be a sacrifice to cleanse us—a covering to wash us. As the psalmist wrote, "Wash away all my iniquity and cleanse me from my sin. . . . Cleanse me with hyssop, and I will be clean; wash me, and I will be whiter than snow" (Psalm 51:2,7). The only way to be cleansed is to be washed by the blood of the Lamb, the Prince of Peace.

The Prince of Peace died on the cross to take the punishment for all your sins—past, present and future. He was your substitute, and He wants to be your Savior. Even though at birth you were not "rubbed with salt" (Ezekiel 16:4), you can now be washed with pure water. Salt is a cleanser and a purifier, and by being washed in the blood of Lamb, you are cleansed and made pure in the eyes of the King. You are made *holy* and *righteous*, and you can stand in His presence with confidence. Better yet, the King *desires* you to stand before Him, for you were created to have intimate fellowship with Him. The Son Himself stands at the door of your heart, deep within the secret place, and knocks (see Revelation 3:20), because both He and the Father want this reunion.

There is only one way for you to have true citizenship in the Kingdom and be clothed in garments of salvation. Paul summed it up this way: "If you confess with your mouth, 'Jesus is Lord,' and believe in your heart that God raised him from the dead, you will be saved. For it is with your heart that you believe and are justified, and it is with your mouth that you confess and are saved" (Romans 10:9-10). It is as simple as that! To accept the King's gift, all you need to do is accept the sacrifice of His Son, the Prince of Peace, and believe that He is your Savior. When you believe these truths by faith, confess them with your mouth, and believe them in your heart, you will be saved. You will receive the cure from the terrible disease of death and be wrapped in cloth—the King's garments of salvation.

Now, I know all the lies that Lucifer, the discourager, wants you to believe. He would like you to believe that you must work for your salvation. But the Word clearly states that you are saved by *grace* and not by *works*. Lucifer would also like you to believe that all roads lead to the King. But the King's own Son declared, "I am the way and the truth and the life. No one comes to the Father except through me" (John 14:6). So, there is nothing you can do on your own that will allow you to enter the kingdom of heaven, because the Prince of Peace, Jesus Christ, did it all.

One of the most wonderful promises of the King is this: "Everyone who calls on the name of the Lord will be saved" (Joel 2:32). Are you ready to do this? Are you ready to accept the gift of salvation? If so, kneel before your Creator, the King. Bow your life to Him in reverence and respect. Pray a prayer from your heart—from the secret place—and call on the name of the King's Son, Jesus Christ. Then repeat after me:

> *My King and my God, I know that I am a sinner. I know that there is nothing I can do on my own to be saved. I believe that You are God. I believe in Your Son, the Prince of Peace, Jesus Christ. I know that You, Jesus, died on the cross for me so that my sins could be washed away. I believe that You rose from the dead. I accept the gift. I receive You, Jesus Christ, as my Lord and my Savior. I accept Your offer of forgiveness and eternal life. My King, I thank You for this wonderful free gift that You have given to me! In Jesus' precious name, Amen.*

If you prayed this prayer, you have received the King's gift, and immeasurable worth has been bestowed upon you. In my future letters, I will describe these unimaginable riches that you have obtained, but know that they are only yours *if you have truly accepted the gift of the King.* If you have still not accepted His gift, you do not yet possess these riches. But don't stop reading! You can have them the moment you desire them. So keep this letter and turn back to it whenever you are ready to accept the King's proposal—when you are ready to accept His Son as your Lord and Savior.

Now, dear beloved—yes, that's right, *beloved*—as you prayed that prayer, you became a citizen of the Kingdom and were adopted into the King's own family. Right now, the King's knights (also known as angels) are rejoicing over you. Will you join them in celebration? Isaiah, another of the King's scribes, declared, "I delight greatly in the LORD; my soul rejoices in my God. For he has clothed me with garments of salvation" (Isaiah 61:10a).

So let the angels hear you shout, *"I am clothed with garments of salvation!"*

Joyfully exclaim, *"I am saved!"*

Proclaim your new identity from the rooftops: *"I am a citizen of the kingdom of heaven!"*

Understand within your heart—deep within your inmost being—that you were created to have intimate fellowship with the King and are His beloved. Let Him hear you cherish it: *"I am His beloved!"*

You are now clothed in garments of salvation, and no one can snatch you out of the King's hand. But be prepared to stand firm against Lucifer, who will come and try to discourage you. Remember, *this is war!* He will remind you of the wrongs you have done in the past and whisper that you are not worthy to be saved. When he does, just remind him that you have been saved by grace and not by anything you have done. No one is worthy of salvation, which is what makes the gift so precious.

In view of the truth, ponder this gift that you have received in the secret place in your heart, for your salvation is one of the treasures that is to be cherished and kept precious. Watch and wait for my next letter, for in it I will explain what it means to be the bride of the Prince! Until that time, remember that the King loves you deeply.

Rejoicing in Him,
Your Willing Servant

Chapter Five

Clothed in Fine Linen

You Are the Bride of Christ

> *I will make you my wife forever,*
> *showing you righteousness and justice,*
> *unfailing love and compassion.*
> *I will be faithful to you and make you mine,*
> *and you will finally know me as LORD.*
> Hosea 2:19-20, NLT

*D*ear Beloved Believer,

As I wrote to you in my previous letter, from the moment you accepted the King's proposal to receive His Son, the Prince of Peace, as your Savior, you were adopted into the King's family. Adoption is an act of love. In fact, during the time that your Prince walked this earth, adoption was considered an act of love by law! Under the Roman rule of the time, it was a legal act sealed in a court of law. The same is still true today. The moment you accepted the Prince, your adoption became a legal act of love in a court of law in heaven. The adoption papers were sealed in the Lamb's own blood, declaring, "Paid in full!"

The King's Word states that another name for the Prince of Peace is "the Bridegroom." This is significant, because when you accepted the King's gift, you not only became His child but also the *bride of Christ*. In order for you to fully understand what this means, I have to tell you about the wedding customs of the Jewish people, for woven within this tradition is a beautiful love story that involves you!

In the Word, we read that the Jews were the King's chosen people. He blessed them by making them into a great nation, and He intended for them to be a blessing to all people on earth (see Genesis 12:2-3). In the same way, He has blessed you by calling you to join His family. In fact, the love He has for you is so deep that He chose you and set you apart from all the other people He created.

In the Jewish culture, it was the father of the bridegroom who picked the bride; and today, God the Father, the King of kings, has chosen you to be the bride of Christ. Remember what the King Himself said through His scribe Ezekiel: "On the day you were born. . . . You were thrown out into the open field, for on the day you were born you were despised. Then I passed by and saw you kicking about in your blood, and as you lay there in your blood I said to you, 'Live!'" (Ezekiel 16:4-6). It was God the Father, the King, who chose you to live. And it was God the Father, the King, who chose you to be His Son's bride.

This custom of the father finding a bride for his son dates to the beginning of time. Back in the Garden of Eden, God the Father created Eve for Adam and "brought her to the man" (Genesis 2:22b). Soon after, you find other fathers finding wives for their sons throughout the book of Genesis in the King's Word. This reveals an amazing fact about you! The King has always been orchestrating events to prepare *you* to become His Son's bride. You have been chosen by the Father to be the bride of the Prince of Peace.

Let me share another wonderful truth for you to ponder in the secret place in your heart: It is *not only* the Father who chose you, but also the Prince Himself who loved you so deeply that He wanted you to be His bride. As He has said, "You did not choose me, but I chose you. . . . As it is, you do not belong to the world, but I have chosen you out of the world" (John 15:16a,19b). Are you beginning to grasp the depth of love that both the Father and the Son have for you?

Once the father chose the bride, the bridegroom would travel from his father's house to the home of his intended. In the same way, the Prince of Peace left His Father's house in heaven to come to earth, the home of His intended bride. As the scribe John writes, "The Word [the Prince of Peace] became flesh and made his dwelling among us. We have seen his glory, the glory of the One and Only, who came from the Father, full of grace and truth" (John 1:14). The Prince of Peace came to earth and made His dwelling here because of His incredible love for you.

After the bridegroom arrived, the father of the bride would negotiate a price that had to be paid for his daughter. This custom, which still exists to this day, is called the "bride price." In the book of Genesis in the King's Word, we read about a man named Shechem who desired to pay such a bride price to wed a woman named Dinah. He said to Dinah's father, "Let me find favor in your eyes, and I will give you whatever you ask. Make the price for the bride and the gift I am to bring as great as you like, and I'll pay whatever you ask me. Only give me the girl as my wife" (Genesis 34:11-12). Although Shechem was not an honorable man, he was willing to pay whatever price the girl's father asked. In the same way, a man named Jacob so loved a woman named Rachel that he gave 14 years of labor to her father to be able to wed her.

While these are impressive stories, the greatest bride price ever paid in history was the one the King of kings was willing to pay to secure you. And because the Bridegroom loves you so deeply, He literally gave up everything to make you His own. The price He paid was the shedding of His blood on a hillside called Calvary. Amazing love!

> For you know that it was not with perishable things such as silver or gold that you were redeemed. . . but with the precious blood of Christ, a lamb without blemish or defect.
>
> —1 Peter 1:18-19

It was not the soldiers who were on the Prince's mind as He walked toward His captors in the Garden of Gethsemane. He had already set His face like flint and determined what He had to do. In fact, it was *you* who was on His mind as He was bound and led through the city of Jerusalem in the dark of night. It was *you* He was concerned about as He was beaten and led to the cross. It was *you*, His bride, whom He was thinking about in love as He walked those final steps and paid the largest bride price in history. He was willing to do it all because you are so precious to Him.

In Jewish culture, negotiating the bride price was a formal, legal proceeding. Perhaps this is the reason why the Prince of Peace, your Bridegroom, was willing to endure a trial at the time of His arrest. This formal proceeding took place before the Sanhedrin, the 71-member Jewish Supreme Court. In truth, as Pastor Jon Courson notes, the trial was a sham, because Mosaic Law forbade the Jewish counsel to meet at night.[1] But the Prince of Peace, the Creator of the Universe, allowed it to occur because of His love for you. Don't overlook this fact. He orchestrated events, and even Jewish wedding tradition, thousands of years before so you would come to understand the depth of His love. Ponder these truths in the secret place in your heart so that you might grasp "how wide and long and high and deep is the love of Christ" (Ephesians 3:18). Those, dear beloved, are the dimensions of the cross. This is an amazing love that surpasses human knowledge.

So it was, with you on His mind, that the Prince of Peace, your Bridegroom, walked willingly to His death. And as He hung in agony on the cross, He cried out in a loud voice, "Tetelestai" (John 19:30). *Tetelestai* is a Greek accounting term that literally means, "It is finished, it has been performed, it is paid."[2] According to Warren Wiersbe, it means "the debt has been paid, it stands paid, and it always will be paid."[3] As a sinner who had broken the King's law, you had a debt that you were unable to pay. But when you turned to the Prince of Peace and accepted His offer of salvation in faith, your sins were forgiven and the debt you owed to the King was cancelled forever. Your Bridegroom, the Prince of Peace, paid your debt in full and performed all of His duties as your groom-to-be.

In Jewish culture, once the bride price was paid, the marriage covenant began. From that moment on, the man and the woman were considered to be husband and wife. Even though the marriage had not yet been consummated, the bride was declared to be "set apart" for her bridegroom. We see this play out in the story of Mary and Joseph in the King's Word. Mary had been set apart for Joseph, which is why when she was found to be with child, Joseph "had in mind to divorce her quietly" (Matthew 1:19). In the same way, the moment you accepted the Prince of Peace, you were set apart for Him and given gifts of immeasurable worth. It is the King's desire that you discover the precious treasure that this truth contains. For this treasure contains your worth—*your worth of who you are in Christ!*

Again, this fascinating truth parallels the marriage traditions in Jewish culture, where the bridegroom would give his bride gifts of clothing and precious jewels. In my last letter, I told you that Your Father, the King, is holy and cannot look upon sin. Therefore, at the moment of your salvation, the King's Son dressed you in fine linen and clothed you in righteousness so that His Father, the King of kings, could look on you in love. In truth, when the King looks at you, it is actually the Bridegroom's righteousness He sees. You have been washed clean by the blood of the Lamb and covered in fine linens of righteousness. It is an ongoing covering, day after day, moment by moment.

In a Jewish wedding, a blessing was proclaimed to the bride, just as a blessing has been proclaimed over you. In fact, the blessing you have received is almost unimaginable to fathom, for it is a blessing from the King Himself! He desires to prosper you and not harm you. He has plans to give you a hope and a future (see Jeremiah 29:11). He has already prepared in advance good works for you to do (see Ephesians 2:10). In view of this, learn the truth of *who you are in Christ* so that you may walk in truth and your life will have true meaning and fulfillment. What more of a blessing could you ask for?

Once the blessing was proclaimed, the bride and the bridegroom drank from a cup and celebrated the betrothal with a feast. Your Bridegroom, the Prince of Peace, symbolized this marriage covenant during the Last Supper, the Passover Supper, with His disciples. What's even more amazing is that you partake of this Last Supper and continue to celebrate your betrothal every time you take communion in remembrance of Him. Listen to what your Prince said: "This cup is the new covenant in my blood; do this, whenever you drink it, in remembrance of me" (1 Corinthians 11:25b).

After all of this took place in the Jewish marriage traditions of old, the bridegroom would leave the home of his bride and return to his father's house. During this time apart, the bridegroom would prepare a place for his bride and himself to live. Once again, this is true of your Bridegroom.

After paying the bride price, the Prince of Peace returned to His Father's home in heaven, and at this very moment He is preparing a place for you to live. How beautiful it must be! We can only imagine it, for the King's Word says:

> No eye has seen, no ear has heard, no mind has conceived what God has prepared for those who love him.
>
> —1 Corinthians 2:9b

Once the bridegroom returned home, it was up to the *father* to decide when his son was ready to get his bride. Neither the bride—nor the bridegroom, for that matter—knew the day or the hour. Sometimes, the father would make them wait as long as a year. When the appointed day finally arrived, the bridegroom and his men would put on festive clothes and prepare for the event. A crown would be placed on the groom's head. Then everyone—the groom, his men, family and friends—would go to surprise the bride. A band of musicians and singers would join them as they traveled. Imagine the joy of the moment! As the groom drew near to the bride's house, he would give a loud shout to announce his arrival. Although the bride expected her bridegroom, she never knew exactly when he would come for her, so she and her maids had to always be ready and prepared.

What makes this account so fascinating is that it parallels the events to come with your Bridegroom. As the Prince Himself has said, "No one knows about that day or hour, not even the angels in heaven, nor the Son, but only the Father" (Matthew 24:36). Just like the brides of old, you must always be ready and prepared for your Bridegroom, for He could arrive at any moment. The King has orchestrated all of the events of the past and the future to prove the depth of His love for you, and the Prince of Peace has given up all to wed you, but you must not be caught unaware when you hear His loud shout. Ponder this truth in the secret place within the depth of your own heart.

The pinnacle of the Jewish wedding ceremony was the moment the bridegroom led his bride and the whole party back to his father's house in a time of celebration. As one of the King's psalmists declared, "The bride, a princess, looks glorious in her golden gown. In her beautiful robes, she is led to the king, accompanied by her bridesmaids. What a joyful and enthusiastic procession as they enter the king's palace!" (Psalm 45:13-15, NLT). The ceremony was celebrated with a large feast, and all of the bride and groom's friends and families were invited to attend.

The pinnacle of your walk as a member of the King's family—in truth, the moment you should be living for and waiting for—will come when you least expect it. You will hear a shout and the sound of a loud trumpet, and you will see your Bridegroom coming on the clouds with a grand procession of His angels in great power and glory. At that moment, you will be caught up to meet the Prince of Peace, your Bridegroom, in the clouds. He will come to take you, His beloved, to the place He has prepared especially for you. As the scribe John records:

> Hallelujah! For the Lord our God the Almighty reigns. Let us rejoice and exalt and give him the glory, for the marriage of the Lamb has come, and his Bride has made herself ready; it was granted her to clothe herself with fine linen, bright and pure—for the fine linen is the righteous deeds of the saints. And the angel said to me, "Write this: Blessed are those who are invited to the marriage supper of the Lamb." And he said to me, "These are the true words of God."
>
> —Revelation 19:6b-9, ESV

In closing, there is one more truth concerning the fine linen that I do not want you to overlook. Note that the passage above states that "the fine linen is the righteous deeds of the saints." There is something to be learned in this statement—something that your Bridegroom, the Prince of Peace, desires you to understand. As you wait for His return, there is a task that you should be busy doing so you will be prepared for when He comes. Wait for my future letters, for in them I will describe more about this task.

Until that time, never forget that the King has chosen you. Let Him hear you ponder this within the secret place: *"I am chosen."*

Yes, you are chosen to be His child, so let Him hear you giggle out loud: *"I am a child of the King."*

The King of kings Himself has blessed you. Worship Him as you embrace it in awe: *"I am blessed."*

As you go forth this day as the bride of the Prince of Peace, walk in truth, knowing who you are in Christ. Let Him hear you shout, *"I am able to walk in truth!"*

Remember that gifts of immeasurable worth have been bestowed on you and that *you* are of worth simply because of who you are in Christ. Let Him hear you accept it, deep within your inmost being: *"I am of worth because of who I am in Christ!"*

You are clothed in fine linen. As His bride, believe it and say, *"I am clothed in the fine linen of His righteousness."*

Cherishing all of this within your heart, never forget that you are set apart in Christ. Let Him hear your whispered "I do" as you accept His hand and say, *"I am the bride of Christ."*

Until He returns,
Your Faithful Attendant

Chapter Six

Clothed in Wisdom

You Are Able to Walk in Wisdom

*For this reason, since the day [I] heard about you,
[I] have not stopped praying for you
and asking God to fill you with the knowledge of his will
through all spiritual wisdom and understanding.*

Colossians 1:9

*D*ear Beloved Believer,

Now that I have established the deep love the King and His Son have for you, it's time to learn more about the fierce battle that surrounds you. It is my prayer, hope and desire that you will understand the truth concerning this battle as written in the King's Word so that you will be victorious. It's important for you to not only have *head knowledge* about this victory, but also *heart knowledge*—the type of knowledge that you apply to your life. (In His Word, the King calls this "wisdom.") I want you to know, as Pastor Warren Wiersbe writes, that "you are not fighting *for* victory, but *from* victory, for Jesus Christ has already defeated Satan!"[1] Your King, who exists outside of time, has already secured the victory over Lucifer, and He had His scribes write down this outcome to encourage you in the battle. For this reason, my precious friend, you can shout, "I am victorious!"

Perhaps you are under the impression that because you have accepted the King as your Lord and Savior and become the bride of Christ, your battle against the enemy will end. Unfortunately, the exact *opposite* is true—the battle *has just begun*. Lucifer, the destroyer, wants you to be ineffective in your walk with the King, and he will attack you at every opportunity. Although you may be young in the knowledge of the King right now, it is my job as the King's servant to train you to walk in maturity so that you will be able to prevail against *all* of the enemy's schemes.

In my previous letters, I drew upon verses from the book of Ezekiel to explain how the King passed by and saw you kicking about in your own blood, which represents your sinful folly. He then brought you to Himself with His lovingkindness and offered to be your Lord and Savior. The moment you decided to accept the King's proposal, He said to you, "Live!" He gave you new life and saved you from your sin. Because you trusted in the King, you are now known as a "believer."

The scribe Ezekiel goes on to explain that the King will now make you "grow like a plant of the field" (Ezekiel 16:7a). The King cares for you so deeply that He will enable you to grow and mature in "the depth of the riches of the wisdom and knowledge of God" (Romans 11:33a). These, dear beloved, are two of the precious treasures the King desires you to cherish in the secret place: knowledge and wisdom.

It is my life's ambition to train you up in knowledge and teach you to apply it so you can walk in wisdom. This is what will prepare you for the plans the King has for you. You will no longer be an infant "tossed back and forth by the waves, and blown here and there by every wind of teaching and by the cunning and craftiness of men in their deceitful scheming. Instead . . . [you] will in all things grow up into him who is the Head, that is, Christ" (Ephesians 4:14-15).

But again, the choice is yours. You can choose to learn the truth and draw closer to the King in wisdom, or you can choose to be led down the path of deceit and fleshly desires. It is my prayer that you will choose "instruction instead of silver [and] knowledge rather than choice gold, for wisdom is more precious than rubies, and nothing you desire can compare with her" (Proverbs 8:10-11).

The first step in growing and maturing in the way of the King is to learn about Lucifer, your enemy, and how to prepare for battle against him. As Paul writes, Lucifer is a cunning foe who will try to deceive you: "But I am afraid that as the serpent deceived Eve by his cunning, your thoughts will be led astray from a sincere and pure devotion to Christ" (2 Corinthians 11:3). For this reason, you need to know exactly who Lucifer is and how you can prevail in spite of his many schemes. As Paul explains:

> Finally, my brethren, be strong in the Lord and in the power of His might. Put on the whole armor of God, that you may be able to stand against the wiles of [Lucifer]. For we do not wrestle against flesh and blood, but against principalities, against powers, against the rulers of the darkness of this age, [and] against spiritual hosts of wickedness in the heavenly places. Therefore take up the whole armor of God, that you may be able to withstand in the evil day, and having done all, to stand.
>
> —Ephesians 6:10-13, NKJV

In future letters I will teach you more concerning this passage—especially about the armor of the King. But for now, I want to focus on Lucifer, the betrayer, because he wants to lead you astray. In truth, the only way you can win this battle is by knowing and understanding your enemy—by being clothed in wisdom. I do not want you to be destroyed from lack of knowledge. This is why I must teach you about him.

As you might have already suspected, Lucifer has many different names. One of his names—which I am sure you have heard the people in the King's court speak of—is Satan, or the devil. In Hebrew, the word *Satan* literally means "accuser,"[2] and in Greek, the *devil*[3] has the same meaning. So we see that Lucifer, your enemy, accuses you day and night before the throne of the King. But remember, my dear precious friend, that even though what Lucifer says may be true, the King in His love has covered you with the blood of His own Son, the Prince of Peace so that you are clothed in righteousness.

Satan also means "adversary,"[4] or one to contend against, because he is the archenemy of the King. And because he is the enemy of the King, he is *your* enemy as well. Lucifer is also known as the tempter. He even tempted the Prince of Peace—so be prepared and realize that he will tempt you. He is the chief sinner. In fact, according to the King's own Word, he "has been sinning from the beginning" (1 John 3:8), and he was "a murderer from the beginning" (John 8:44b). He is the father of all lies—that too is one of his names—and "when he lies, he speaks his native language" (John 8:44c). In other places in the King's Word he is compared to a serpent and a roaring lion (see 2 Corinthians 11:3; 1 Peter 5:8). He is known as the god of this age (see 2 Corinthians 4:4), for he is the unseen power behind all unbelief and ungodliness. However, perhaps his most effective disguise is as an *angel of light* (see 2 Corinthians 11:14).

Lucifer is powerful and not to be taken lightly, but do not despair, my beloved, for your King is much more powerful. In fact, the King has also been given many wonderful names. He is known as the Alpha and the Omega, the

First and the Last, the Almighty God, the King of Glory—among many others—and His attributes far outweigh those of Lucifer. The King is known as your protector, your strength, your fortress, your deliverer, your rock, your shield, your salvation and your stronghold. And do not forget that He calls you His beloved. Therefore, give Him the glory:

> Now to the King eternal, immortal, invisible, the only God, be honor and glory for ever and ever. Amen.
> —1 Timothy 1:17

Now, to overcome Lucifer, you need to know a few important facts about him. First, it is believed that in the King's original creation, Lucifer was the morning star, or son of the dawn. In one version of the King's Word, the Hebrew for "morning star" was translated as "Lucifer," which gives us the source of his name. According to Warren Wiersbe, many believe that Lucifer was "cast down [from heaven] because of his pride and desire to occupy the King's throne."⁵ This is why he is known as a traitor throughout the Kingdom.

A crucial point that you must not overlook is that Lucifer is a *created* being, not *eternal* like your King. He is limited in his knowledge, not all-knowing like your Savior. He is *limited* in his activity, not *all-powerful* like your Lord. He is even *limited* in that he can only be in one place at one time, not *omnipresent* (everywhere-present), like your King. Did you notice the word I repeated again and again? *Limited!* Lucifer is *limited* and has boundaries—never forget that. Do not make him to be something bigger than he is, for that is just what he wants you to do. At the same time, to live your life as if he does *not* exist is also playing into his hands. Either of these two extremes is dangerous to your walk. So, given this, it is of strategic importance to have true knowledge of who he is and how he operates. For even though his powers are limited, since the time of the Fall he has been given rule over the earth. Thus, another name to describe him is "the prince of this world" (John 12:31).

At this point you may be thinking, *If Lucifer is limited, how is he able to accomplish so many things in different parts of the world?* Once again, remember that "we do not wrestle against flesh and blood, but against principalities, against powers, against the rulers of the darkness of this age, [and] against spiritual hosts of wickedness in the heavenly places" (Ephesians 6:12, NKJV). These *principalities, powers, rulers* and *spiritual hosts* are Lucifer's warriors. In fact, Lucifer has a vast army of demonic beings that assist him in his attacks against citizens of the Kingdom. This is why we all struggle as we do.

As I mentioned previously, one of the King's scribes, the apostle John, stated that when Lucifer rebelled against the King, he took one-third of the King's angels with him (see Revelation 12:3-9). Furthermore, Daniel, another of the King's scribes, explained that Lucifer's fallen angels struggle against the King's angels for control of the affairs of nations (see Daniel 10:20-21). Unfortunately, many times you and I are caught in the middle of this battle.

With this in mind, it is important to learn about the *principalities*, for they are the fallen angels—or demonic entities—that have been given power over specific areas of the world. In looking at the Greek word for "principalities" *(arche),* we learn that they are "designated according to their *classes of rank*,"[6] so we know they are highly trained and or-ganized with military precision. Fortunately, in the book that Daniel wrote, we are given some insights as to who these *principalities* are. This is crucial information—top-secret intelligence—that will enable you to walk in wisdom.

Daniel relates how one time he was fasting and praying but no answer came from the King. It was not until three weeks had passed that he learned that the King had in fact dispatched an angel with the answer to his prayer, but that this angel had been detained. The angel described his ordeal to Daniel: "The prince of the Persian kingdom resisted me twenty-one days. Then Michael, one of the chief princes, came to help me, because I was detained there with the king of Persia" (Daniel 10:13). The "prince" of this Persian kingdom was apparently one of Lucifer's warriors who exerted a certain amount of influence over the region. This demon was strong enough to delay the messenger sent by the King, but he could not detain Michael, who is described as the great prince who protects the people of God.[7]

This passage in Daniel indicates that these *principalities* are more active in certain areas of the world. Perhaps you have experienced being in a place where it felt as if something dark and oppressive was there, but you weren't able to explain what it was. If so, you were sensitive to the *principalities* and their influence over that region. I myself have felt this many times during my travels—especially when I am in Eastern Europe. We truly do not wrestle against flesh and blood, but against *principalities*.

While all of this sounds frightening, the purpose of my letter is not to provoke fear in you but to clothe you in wisdom. With this in mind, I want you to know that the King Himself will protect you. Take comfort in knowing that "greater is He who is in you than he who is in the world" (1 John 4:4, NASB). Just listen to the wonderful words penned by David: "For the LORD loves the just and will not forsake his faithful ones. They will be protected forever" (Psalm 37:28).

With this in mind, let's continue your military training, for it is critical that you understand the second regiment of Lucifer's warriors, called the *powers*. These *powers* represent the demonic forces that keep people in bondage.

In the Greek, the word is *exousias*, which could be translated as "force, influence, token of control, power or strength."[8] These demonic forces keep people in bondage by influencing and controlling their lives. However, as I have told you, from the moment of your salvation these *powers* no longer have any authority over you. You are now under the authority of the King of kings!

Many people ask whether a believer can be "demon-possessed." The answer is an emphatic *no*. It is impossible because you are the temple of the King, and the Royal Counselor, also known as the Holy Spirit, *dwells in you*. Listen to what Paul wrote: "If any man destroys the temple of God, God will destroy him, for the temple of God is holy, and that is what you are" (1 Corinthians 3:17, NASB). John writes, "But he who has been born of God keeps himself, and the wicked one does not *touch* him" (1 John 5:18, NKJV, emphasis added). The word "touch" in the Greek could actually be translated "attach."[9] Therefore, it is impossible, according the King's own Word, for a believer to be demon-possessed, because both Lucifer and his powers are unable to *attach* themselves to a child of the King.

However, while a child of the King cannot be possessed, he or she *can* be deceived, tempted, oppressed, afflicted, influenced and manipulated by Lucifer and his *powers*. These demonic *powers* can *deceive* believers into believing a lie, *tempt* them to make decisions contrary to the King's will, *oppress* them from walking in victory, *afflict* them physically (though not all affliction is from Lucifer), *influence* them to remain immature and carnal (instead of mature and Spirit-filled), and *manipulate* them to keep them slaves to sin. Perhaps there has been a time in your life when you fell prey to one or more of these schemes from Lucifer and his cohorts.

Yet once again, remember that you have a choice. You can choose to be a carnal believer and live your life seeking worldly pleasures, which will set you up for remaining in bondage to sin and never completely being all the King desires you to be. Or you can choose to be a victorious, Spirit-filled citizen of the Kingdom who *believes* and *applies* the Word, knowing deep within the secret place—deep within your inmost being—that you are more than a conqueror.

Dear beloved, know that even if you have been living the life of a carnal believer, today is the day you can have victory! These promises of being more than a conqueror and being set free are true. All you need to do is move that knowledge from your head to your heart. This will give you heart knowledge, which, as I have said, is knowledge *applied* to your life.

There is another extremely important truth that I must teach you to enable you to be this Spirit-filled believer. From the moment of your salvation, you not only have the Royal Counselor, the Holy Spirit, dwelling within you, but you also have access to His dynamic power from on high. This dynamic power is what will enable you to walk in wisdom. You cannot be victorious in your own strength—it is an absolute impossibility. You need the power of the Royal Counselor, and you can obtain this power simply by asking the King for it. In my next letter I will show you how to be clothed with His power, but for now I must continue to teach you how Lucifer and his cohorts operate.

For both the unsaved (those who do not have a personal relationship with the King) and carnal believers (those who live to fulfill their fleshly desires and feelings), the demonic *powers* of Lucifer can be extremely destructive. They can keep these individuals in such bondage that they believe there is no hope of escape. Perhaps there is someone you know who is in bondage to sin. Perhaps it is the sin of alcohol abuse, drug abuse, gambling, pornography, wrong relationships or any other sin that is destroying this person's life and the lives of his or her loved ones. These *powers* have this person shackled and chained, and you may fear that he or she will never be set free.

But take heart, for in reading the Word we learn that the King and His Son truly are much stronger than these *powers*. In Luke 13:11, we find the story of a woman "who had been crippled by a spirit for eighteen years. She was bent over and could not straighten up at all." This woman had a demonic *power* over her and did not have the strength on her own to stand firm. But the Prince of Peace set this woman free!

The same can be true in your loved one's life. Keep this person in prayer day and night. Remember that you *do not wrestle against flesh and blood. . . . but against powers*. It is not your family member, your co-worker, your neighbor or your loved one whom you are truly struggling against, but against the demonic *powers* behind that person. It is important for you to realize that your loved one or friend could truly be in bondage. If you do not recognize this, you will be fighting the wrong battle, which is exactly what Lucifer wants you to do!

The truth is that Lucifer, the god of this age, has blinded this person's mind. If this person is unsaved, the only way for him or her to be victorious and overcome Lucifer is to accept the King's Son and be washed in the blood of the Lamb. If this person is a carnal believer, then he or she must *believe* and *apply* the truth of the King's Word through the dynamic power of the Royal Counselor. This battle will only be won through prayer. So keep on praying, and never give up.

Now, to continue your training, I want to tell you about yet a third regiment of Lucifer's warriors. These are *the rulers of the darkness of this age*. These *rulers* exist in our world system and in our culture. In fact, this phrase could also be translated from the Greek as "the rulers of this sinful world."[10] Remember, dear beloved, that Lucifer thinks up the lie, the world sells the lie, and the flesh—when we are not walking victoriously—buys the lie. Have you ever wondered how Lucifer influences the world to buy his lies? It is through these demonic forces, *the rulers of the darkness of this age*. They are the demonic spiritual forces that work in our world system, in our culture, in the political system, in the entertainment industry, in the music industry, in the educational system and in all of the other systems around us.

Think about it. Look, for example, at the "safe sex" lie. This is a deception of Lucifer that states a person can have safe sex outside of marriage by using a condom—that it will protect a person from a sexually transmitted disease or an unwanted pregnancy. But this is *not* the truth; it is a lie that has been sold by our world system. As Dr. Helen Kaplan notes, "It is most important for you to realize that even though condoms have been widely advertised as providing safe sex for women, at this writing not a single study has been published demonstrating that in real life condoms protect women, or men for that matter, against AIDS."[11] Just look at who is involved in spreading this lie: the government, the education system, the medical industry and the entertainment industry, to name just a few. The *rulers of the darkness of this age* have encouraged our world system into selling this lie—a lie that can literally end in death—and many people have bought it.

How I wish I had known this truth when I was younger! When I was at a vulnerable place in my life, I believed so many lies—lies that almost destroyed me. Never forget that these lies represent a demonic attack. Train yourself to be aware and on the lookout for the deceptions that Lucifer and his cohorts try to spread. Be clothed in wisdom so you can grow and mature into a Spirit-filled believer who is walking victoriously through life—a life that has true meaning.

The final regiment on which you must be trained and prepared to fight are the demonic warriors. These are the *spiritual hosts of wickedness in the heavenly places*, and they seek to blind people to the truth of the King's Word. This is exactly what occurred in the Garden of Eden. Listen to the words of Lucifer, the slanderer, as he spoke to Eve: "You will not surely die . . . for God knows that when you eat of it [the tree of the knowledge of good and evil] your eyes will be opened, and you will be like [the King], knowing good and evil" (Genesis 3:4-5).

Let's compare this lie to some of the false teachings we find in the world today. First, there is the lie that all roads lead to heaven. Those who believe this lie say it does not matter which religion you follow, for there is one King and all are worshiping Him in their own way. Once again, this is *not* the truth—it is a lie. Again, as the King's Son, your Prince of Peace, said, "I am the way and the truth and the life. No one comes to the Father except through me" (John 14:6).

If you believe this lie—that all roads lead to heaven—you have a big problem, because it directly contradicts the King's Word. So, I ask, who is lying? Is the Prince of Peace lying when He says there is only one way to the King? No! One of His names is the Truth. You now know the truth, and that truth has set you free (see John 8:32). It is Lucifer, the deceiver, who is once again lying to you by whispering, *"You will not surely die*, for all roads lead to heaven." Sadly, all who believe this lie will be separated from the King after death and be eternally condemned. They will not partake in the everlasting life the King offers. This is why it is crucial for you to learn to rightly divide the Word and discern the truth from the deceptions.

Dear beloved, Lucifer cannot snatch you out of the King's hand, but he can try to keep you from growing into a mature Spirit-filled believer. One of the ways he will do this is by bombarding you with false teachings. Some of the false teachers he employs will even claim that an angel from heaven came to them with another gospel—a gospel different from the Word. In truth, these false teachers really *did* see an angel, for as we know, Lucifer's most effective disguise is as an angel of light. But listen to these words of wisdom from Paul:

> I am astonished that you are so quickly deserting the one who called you by the grace of Christ and are turning to *a different gospel*—which is really no gospel at all. Evidently some people are throwing you into confusion and are trying to pervert the gospel of Christ. But even if we or *an angel from heaven* should preach a gospel other than the one we preached to you, *let him be eternally condemned!*
> —Galatians 1:6-8 (emphasis added)

Powerful words! This teaching shows us that even back in Paul's time, there were *hosts of wickedness* who sought to blind people's eyes to the truth of the King's Word. Paul needed to remind the Galatians that even if an angel from heaven came and preached another gospel, they had been trained to recognize the truth of the gospel of Christ, the King's one and only Son. Remember that your *struggle is not against flesh and blood* and that those who are spreading the lie are not the problem—they are just being deceived. The problem comes from *the spiritual hosts of wickedness in the heavenly places* whom the deceived have allowed to manipulate them.

This is why it is vitally important for you to be trained for battle. My prayer is that you will wait with eager anticipation for my next letters, for they will contain strategic battle wisdom. Until that time, remember that "you are not fighting *for* victory, but *from* victory."[12] Stand firm and believe it as you claim, *"I am victorious!"*

It is because of the King's strength that you are able to grow and walk in maturity. So move forward as you state it: *"I am able to grow and walk in maturity."*

The King protects you at all times as you walk through life. So feel secure as you embrace it: *"I am protected by the King."*

Because of the blood of the Lamb, you are able to overcome sin. You are more than a conqueror. Stand tall as you accept it: *"I am more than a conqueror."*

From the moment of your salvation, you were set free. So ponder this truth deep within your heart as you declare, *"I am set free."*

By cherishing this truth in the secret place in the depth of your own heart, you are able to walk in wisdom. So consider this deep within as you live this truth out in your life: *"I am able to walk in wisdom."*

Be prepared for daily battle by studying and applying the Word. This is vitally important, for it will give you the knowledge and wisdom you need to help you to stand firm. Learn these things "in order that Satan might not outwit [you]. For [now you] are not unaware of his schemes" (2 Corinthians 2:11). Always remember that you are clothed in wisdom and that wisdom is the key to being victorious.

Standing firm in spite of Lucifer's schemes,
Your Trustworthy Attendant

Chapter Seven

Clothed with Power

You Are Empowered by the Holy Spirit

And behold, I am sending the promise
of my Father upon you.
But stay in the city until you are
clothed with power from on high.
Luke 24:49, ESV

Dear Beloved Believer,

In a previous letter, I told you that your Bridegroom, the Prince of Peace, is preparing a place for you and that one day He will return to claim you. Now, as you wait for His return, are you reading His messages of love found within the Word? Do you know what your Bridegroom's final words were before He ascended to the Father in heaven? Do you desire to know?

It is important for you to know the Prince's final statements before He left the earth because they reveal two important truths in your life as a believer. The first truth is that you have been given a gift that contains the power and strength you need to walk victoriously. In fact, it is impossible to walk worthy of your calling without this powerful gift. The second truth is that you have been given a mission to complete as you await His return. In view of these truths, I present a challenge to you—a challenge to learn and understand the final words your Prince had to say.

Let's look at the first truth, which contains the gift you have been given. Before your Prince left this world, He told His followers, "I am going to send you what my Father has promised; but stay in the city until you have been clothed with power from on high" (Luke 24:49). What was this power from on high? As I mentioned in a previous letter, there is only One True God who by nature is evident in three persons: God the Father (the King), Jesus the Son (the Prince of Peace), and the Holy Spirit (the Royal Counselor). It is this third person, the Royal Counselor, whom the King out of His love has sent to help you in every situation of your life.

There are many wonderful names attributed to this third person. He is known as the Holy Spirit, the Spirit of Truth, the Promised One, the Dynamic Power, the Helper, the Comforter, the Teacher and the Companion who will abide with you always. But perhaps the name that describes Him best is the Royal Counselor. The word "royal" is derived from the Holy Spirit being of regal status and power, for He is sovereign. The word "counselor" is attributed to Him based on something your Prince said: "I will ask the Father, and he will give you another Counselor to be with you forever" (John 14:16). In the Greek, the word "counselor" is *parakletos*. According to Pastor Chuck Smith, when this word is broken down, we find that "*para* is the Greek preposition for 'with' or 'alongside of,' while *kletos* is the word for 'called.'"[1] Therefore, *parakletos* literally means "one called alongside to help."[2]

You have been given this sovereign power because of who you are in Christ. Remember, you are royalty. Before He left the earth, the Prince of Peace told His followers, "It is for your good that I am going away. Unless I go away, the Counselor will not come to you; but if I go, I will send him to you" (John 16:7). He knows that the battle is fierce and that you are unable to stand in your own strength, so He returned to the right hand of the King and gave you the Royal Counselor as His gift of power and protection. Now, you are truly able to stand "strong in the Lord and in the power of His might" (Ephesians 6:10, NJKV). But take heed: you can't do this on your own.

It is interesting to note that the Royal Counselor has the same attributes as both the King and the Prince of Peace. He is *eternal*, for He has no beginning and no end. He is *omniscient*, for He knows all things. He is *omnipresent*, for He is everywhere at all times. He is *omnipotent*, because He has absolute, infinite, sovereign power. In fact, it was His power that raised the Prince of Peace, Jesus Christ, from the dead! As Pastor Smith goes on to say, the Royal Counselor is "God Himself, a Person with whom you can enjoy a personal relationship. He is not merely an impersonal force or power or essence within the universe."[3] In view of this truth, you can rely on Him regardless of what you are facing, for He too loves you deeply and will never abandon you. Lucifer, the father of all lies, has deceived anyone who believes anything less of Him.

There are three distinct Greek prepositions used in the New Testament of the King's Word that relate to the Royal Counselor: *para, en* and *epi*. The Greek word *para* means that the Royal Counselor is *with* you, and it could also be translated that He is *beside* you.[4] As the scribe John records, your Prince used this word for the Royal Counselor when speaking to His followers:

> The world cannot accept [the Royal Counselor], because it neither sees him nor knows him. But you know him, for he lives *with* [*para*] you and will be in you.
>
> —John 14:17, emphasis added

The Royal Counselor, just like the King of kings and the Prince of Peace, is a person who desires to speak to you and hear from you. He desires to guide you, help you, strengthen you and teach you. In fact, He desires to have a real, intimate, personal relationship *with* you. He is the one who wants to meet *with* you in the secret place, deep within your inmost being in your heart. He wants to be *beside* you and help you in your life. This is why I have written this letter to you, for it is vitally important that you come to know the person of the Holy Spirit, the Royal Counselor, and know Him in His fullness.

The Greek word *en* means that the Royal Counselor is *in* you. He has been *in* you from the moment of your salvation. In fact, you are His dwelling place—His temple. As Paul writes in the Word:

> Do you not know that your body is a temple of the Holy Spirit, who is *in* [*en*] you, whom you have received from God? You are not your own; you were bought at a price. Therefore honor God with your body.
> —1 Corinthians 6:19-20, emphasis added

According to Pastor Smith, "The primary work of the Spirit in the life of every believer is to conform him or her into the image of Christ. Everything He does in our lives is intended to serve this goal."[5] This is why He is also known as the Revealer, for He "makes known through divine inspiration" all that the King created you to be.[6] Unlike Lucifer, who will reveal your failures in order to condemn you, the Royal Counselor will reveal areas where you "missed the mark" to encourage you and enable you to fulfill the King's purpose for your life. Some call this "revealing conviction"—the "state of being convinced of error or compelled to admit the truth."[7]

So it is that the Spirit of Truth, the Royal Counselor, will guide you to the truth so you can see the error of your ways and become more and more like your beloved Prince of Peace. He will help you live in righteousness, which is "hitting the mark."[8] So take heart. Walk worthy of your calling and do not allow Lucifer, the discourager, to cause you to think that conviction is a terrible thing.

Perhaps the most important of the three Greek prepositions used in association with the Royal Counselor is *epi*. *Epi* means "to come upon or on you,"[9] and it describes how He will fill you to overflowing with His dynamic power. It was for this power that your Prince instructed His followers to wait—it was what they needed so they could carry out "the righteous deeds of the saints" (Revelation 19:8b, ESV). Remember, there is something you are to be busy about as you are awaiting your Bridegroom's return. This is why He urged them:

> Do not leave Jerusalem, but wait for the gift my Father promised, which you have heard me speak about. For John baptized with water, but in a few days you will be baptized with the Holy Spirit. . . . But you will receive power when the Holy Spirit comes *on* [*epi*] you; and you will be my witnesses in Jerusalem, and in all Judea and Samaria, and to the ends of the earth.
> —Acts 1:4b-5,8, emphasis added

There are many different terms that have been coined to describe how a person receives this gift. Some refer to it as the "baptism of the Holy Spirit," others label it as being "filled with the Spirit," and still others say they "received the Holy Spirit." What you call it is not important—what matters is that you receive the promised Holy Spirit, the Royal Counselor, so you can be clothed with power.

Now, it is important to know that Lucifer, the thief, does not want you to have this gift, for it will give you far greater power than anything he has. For this reason, he will try to convince you that you do not need to receive it. He has actually been quite successful in this regard, for he has been able to cause much confusion in churches about the Royal Counselor. Nevertheless, I like what Henry Gainey has to say: "If a doctrine is mentioned in the gospels, occurs in the book of Acts and is taught in the epistles, we can rest assured that it is a proper practice for the church."[10] With this in mind, give any confusion and fear you might encounter over to the King. "For the promise is to you and to your children, and to all who are afar off, as many as the Lord our God will call" (Acts 2:39, NKJV).

Perhaps you are wondering how you receive this marvelous empowering of the Holy Spirit. It is simple: by *faith*. As you study the Word, you will discover that some received the gift through prayer and the laying on of hands, while others received it simply by hearing the Word. Either way, it was received by faith. As John writes, "This is the confidence we have in approaching God: that if we ask anything according to his will, he hears us" (1 John 5:14). Since you know that the Prince's final words to His disciples were to wait for the power of the Holy Spirit to come upon them, you can know that it is His will for you to receive it as well. He is the same yesterday, today and forever. So, if you have never received this gift, pray the following from your heart:

> *Lord, I thank You for this promised gift. I receive now the gift of Your Spirit [the Royal Counselor] in my life, along with the power to transform and to change me. I ask that Your power might flow forth from my life to help and to strengthen others around me. Bless them through me by bestowing on them Your love and Your power. In Jesus' name I pray, Amen.[11]*

If you said this prayer in faith, know that regardless of what you may feel, you have received the King's gift. As

Gainey goes on to say, "The baptism [of the Spirit] is received by faith, just as salvation is received by faith. Many who are saved have a dramatic emotional experience, accompanied by joy, weeping, or tremendous peace. Others who are saved often confess that they felt nothing at the time: no emotional experience. Those who 'felt nothing' are just as saved as those who had a dramatic experience. . . . The same is true with the baptism of the Holy Spirit. . . . [It is] received by faith, not blind faith, but faith based on fact."[12]

There is really only one outward sign that reveals itself if you truly have received this wonderful gift. Look again at what the Prince of Peace said:

> But you will receive power when the Holy Spirit comes
> on you; and you will be my *witnesses*.
> —Acts 1:8a, emphasis added

The Prince of Peace, Jesus Christ, said that you would be His *witness*. This is what He desires you to be busy about as you wait for His return. This is what He wants you to live out in your life over time. Being a *witness* is the fine linen and "righteous deeds of the saints" of which John wrote about in the book of Revelation. This is one of the reasons why you were given life!

Now, do not worry about how to be this witness. The Royal Counselor has been given to guide you and to teach you. As Pastor Smith states, "Being a witness is more than speaking words; it is living a life. The word *witness* comes from the Greek word *martus*, which transliterated into English is *martyr*. We think of a martyr as one who dies for his faith; however, it is really one whose life is so totally committed to his faith that nothing will dissuade him from it, not even the threat of death. His death does not make him a martyr; it only confirms that he was truly a martyr."[13] Actions speak louder than words. As you live out your new life, the words will easily follow. In fact, you may be surprised at just how easily they flow from you.

So, as Paul wrote, "Be strong in the Lord and in the power of His might" (Ephesians 6:10, NKJV). Receive the King's gift and be filled with the dynamic power of the Holy Spirit, your Royal Counselor. Allow the King to use you to be His witness. Remember that you are the temple of the Holy Spirit. Let Him hear you state it: *"I am the temple of the Holy Spirit."*

Never forget that you are clothed with power from on high. Say it with strength: *"I am clothed with power."*

Understand in your heart that out of the King's glorious riches He has empowered you by the Holy Spirit. So shout it out loud: *"I am empowered by the Holy Spirit."*

In view of this truth, you are His witness, for this is one of the reasons why you were given life. So allow your actions to speak out this truth in your life. Live it as you proclaim it: *"I am His witness."*

Until my next letter, remember that you are able to walk worthy of your calling because of this wonderful empowering gift. So shout it with joy: *"I am able to walk worthy of my calling."*

I close with these words from Paul: "May the grace of the Lord Jesus Christ, and the love of God, and the fellowship of the Holy Spirit be with you all" (2 Corinthians 13:14).

Living for Him by power from on high,
Your Willing Witness

Chapter Eight

Girded with the Belt of Truth

You Are Able to Stand Firm

Therefore take up the whole armor of God,
that you may be able to withstand in the evil day. . . .
Stand therefore, having girded your waist with truth.
Ephesians 6:13-14a, NKJV

*D*ear Beloved Believer,

Now that I have told you about Lucifer and his warriors and the power that the Royal Counselor provides to you, it is time for me to teach you how to be clothed in the proper battle attire so you can withstand the enemy's attacks. Remember, victory can never come by relying on your own power. If you try to win the battle on your own strength, you will just fail. However, when you allow the Royal Counselor to equip you, you will be able to "put on the whole armor of God, that you may be able to stand against the wiles of the devil" (Ephesians 6:11, NKJV).

As you grow and mature in the ways of the King, Lucifer will try to get you off course and cause you to be ineffective. He will use different tactics to make you stumble and fall. In fact, there will be many times when you will want to just give up the good fight. But take heart, for the equipment the King has designed will protect you from Lucifer's many methods of warfare and allow you to stand firm and be victorious. Recognizing the traitor's tactics and using the appropriate armor will enable you to successfully defend yourself in battle.

I must admit that when I was a young believer, I had no idea what the armor was or how to use it. In fact, I was not even aware there *was* any armor. Later, as I grew and matured in the ways of the King, I still had no idea that I was in the middle of a battlefield and that a war was waging all around me. It wasn't until later when someone shared with me what was truly taking place within the spiritual realm and how that was affecting the struggles I was having that everything began to change for the better. Perspective changes everything!

The King does not want you to be unaware of your situation. He is training you for a special work. He loves you deeply, and nothing will be able to separate you from that love. However, the only way you will be able to do the work He is calling you to do is by being fully trained and prepared. So, with this in mind, let's begin to look at each of the seven pieces of armor the King has provided. We will begin with the *belt of truth*, which is the foundational piece of armor.

When Paul wrote the book of Ephesians, he was being held in a Roman prison, and the belt about which he wrote was modeled on those worn by Roman soldiers. Now, it might seem strange to you that one of the King's own scribes would end up in prison. It must have seemed like a devastating blow from the enemy, and many probably wondered, *Where is the King? Why is He not rescuing Paul?* But in fact, it was the King Himself who was orchestrating the events in Paul's life, because what Lucifer intended for evil the King intended for good. So the King allowed Paul to be imprisoned so He could inspire him to write down this crucial training material. The King knew, in His love for you, that you would need the information that Paul would write about.

But getting back to the belt—the one the Roman soldier wore was not like the narrow belts with which we are familiar today. It was a leather apron, much like a skirt, that covered just below mid-thigh and helped protect the lower part of the soldier's body. The solider first attached his sword and his breastplate to the belt, and as he secured each additional piece of armor to it, it gave him the inner strength he needed to enter the battle. The belt was so valuable to a soldier that it was worthy to be prized along with silver.

The belt of truth should be just as highly prized in your life, for it represents the knowledge of the King's Word. But remember, it is not enough to simply have head knowledge about what the Word says; you need heart knowledge—that which you *believe* and *apply* to your life. It is not enough to just carry the Word around with you wherever you go. Like the Roman soldier's belt, it must surround, encircle and fully encompass every aspect of your life. The belt of truth speaks of a life that is secure, a life that has foundation, and a life in which the applied Word governs actions and motives. This is why it is vitally important that you read the King's Word daily.

In Paul's day, the Roman soldier wore a long flowing tunic, much like a robe, that reached down to his ankles. "Girding your waist" literally meant to tuck the loose ends of the soldier's tunic into his belt to prepare for the running he would have to do either in battle or in service. With this picture in mind, you can see how the belt was such a foundational piece of armor! It kept the soldier from stumbling and falling.

There is much wisdom you can learn from this picture. You must also *gird up* and *tuck in* the loose ends of your life. You must get them in line with the foundation of the King's

Word so you will be prepared to run the race, fight the battle and serve the King. It is only by allowing the Word to fully encompass your life—by knowing and applying it—that you will be victorious. Just like the Roman soldier's belt, your belt of truth, the King's Word, is the foundation that will keep you from stumbling and falling.

The word "gird" also means "to prepare oneself for action."[1] Just as the Roman solider prepared his tunic for physical battle, you must prepare your heart and mind for spiritual battle. You do this by eliminating any thoughts or habits that hinder your walk with the King. Listen to what another of the King's scribes wrote:

> Therefore *gird up the loins of your mind*, be sober, and rest your hope fully upon the grace that is to be brought to you at the revelation of Jesus Christ.
> —1 Peter 1:13, NKJV, emphasis added

To "gird up the loins of your mind" simply means to be spiritually alert and prepare yourself through knowledge of the King's Word. In view of this, you need to establish in your mind a highly esteemed view of the Word. Never forget that Lucifer will twist the Word just enough to cause you to doubt. He will also try to convince you that there are some problems with the Word. The only way that you will be able to stand against the onslaught of Lucifer and his cohorts is by knowing and understanding that the King's Word is *inspired, inerrant* and *infallible.*

Allow me to explain each of these terms. First, *inspired* means that the King Himself communicated His message directly to individuals who wrote His words down. The King is known as Jehovah-Elohim, "the Eternal Creator," and He is the all-knowing God of the universe. What He inspires is absolute truth. As He said to His scribe Isaiah, "I am the LORD, and there is no other. . . . I, the LORD, speak the truth" (Isaiah 45:18b-19). Furthermore, as Paul wrote, "All Scripture is God-breathed and is useful for teaching, rebuking, correcting and training in righteousness, so that the man of God may be thoroughly equipped for every good work" (2 Timothy 3:16-17). The scribe Peter added, "Above all, you must understand that no prophecy of Scripture came about by the prophet's own interpretation. For prophecy never had its origin in the will of man, but men spoke from God as they were carried along by the Holy Spirit" (2 Peter 1:20-21).

I have already told you that there are 66 different books written by 40 different scribes in the King's Word, but did you know that these books were written over a 1,600-year period? Listen to what Sylvia Charles says about this: "Kings and princes, poets and philosophers, prophets and states-men, shepherds, doctors and fishermen were all inspired by the Holy Spirit to write."[2] As you study the Word each day, you will come to understand that there is no humanly way possible that it was written without inspiration of the King. But again, because of the King's great love for you, you have a choice: you can choose to read the Word and gain vital knowledge, or you can choose not to read it. But I must warn you: if you choose to *not* read the Word daily, you are laying aside a foundational piece of armor—your belt of truth—and leaving yourself vulnerable to Lucifer's attacks.

When the King's Word is described as *inerrant*, it means that it is without error. Simply put, it means that the origi-nal scribes did not write down the wrong message. Listen to what one of the King's scribes wrote: "Every word of God is flawless; he is a shield to those who take refuge in him" (Proverbs 30:5). Ponder this verse deep within your heart so that when the battle is raging and those around you are say-ing the Word is not the truth, you can take refuge in your King and know His Book is without error. Take comfort in the fact that the King Himself promises that "no weapon formed against you shall prosper" (Isaiah 54:17a, NKJV). His Word is flawless.

Finally, *infallible* means that the King's Word is not only *without* error, but it is actually *incapable* of error. Listen to what the psalmist David wrote:

> The law of the LORD is perfect, reviving the soul. The statutes of the LORD are trustworthy, making wise the simple. The precepts of the LORD are right, giving joy to the heart. The commands of the LORD are radiant, giving light to the eyes. . . . They are more precious than gold, than much pure gold; they are sweeter than honey, than honey from the comb. By them is your servant warned; in keeping them there is great reward.
>
> —Psalm 19:7-8,10-11

Be prepared! The counsel of friends, though often well-meaning, can lead you astray. Even fellow believers of the King can give misguided counsel. Always rely on the precepts of the King, for they are right and just and will bring joy to your heart. Everything in life must be weighed and balanced by the King's Word, for it is perfect and true and it will revive your soul when you do not know which way to turn.

When you believe and trust in the solid foundation of the Word, you will be able to walk in integrity. The word "integrity" means "complete or undivided," and this is what the Word does—it focuses your mind so that it is secure and unwavering.[3] The belt of truth thus represents a heart, mind and life that is girded together, certain and stable, and ready to serve in any capacity. So allow it to fully encompass your life. Base your daily decisions on the truth found on the pages of the King's Word. Use the truth you find within as your measuring rod, and allow that truth to sink into your heart. As the psalmist wrote to the King:

> Surely you desire truth in the inner parts; you teach me wisdom in the inmost place.
>
> —Psalm 51:6

It is in the secret place, in the depths of your inmost being, that the King desires to teach you wisdom. When the Word pierces your heart, your mind and your life, you will begin to make an impact on others for His Kingdom. Those around you are watching, and sometimes your life will be the *only example of the Word* they will read. So let your actions speak louder than words, and let your life itself be the witness that your Prince of Peace spoke about before He ascended to heaven. Always remember that this is what you are to be busy about as you await His return.

So now, beloved believer, I ask you gird up your heart with the truth of the King's Word and know that nothing can separate you from His love. Embrace this love as you shout out loud, *"I am unable to be separated from the love of the King!"*

Gird up your mind with the truth that you are able to fight the good fight in the strength of the promised Holy Spirit, your Royal Counselor. Let this truth encircle your mind as you claim it: *"I am able to fight the good fight."*

Gird up your life as you walk in integrity. Decide today as you grandly state it, *"I am able to walk in integrity."*

Allow the power of the Holy Spirit, the Promised One, to overflow your life. Realize it and boldly proclaim it: *"I am strong in the Lord and in the power of His might."*

In view of all this, stand tall as you shout, *"I am able to stand firm!"*

Wait eagerly for my next letter, for in it I will share the most beautiful of jewels that have been bestowed to you. Until that time, never forget *who you are in Christ*, for it is not about you, but all about Him, the One and Only, the Prince of Peace.

Walking in integrity,
Your Steadfast Soldier

Chapter Nine

Wearing the Most Beautiful of Jewels

You Are Forgiven

*You grew up and developed and became
the most beautiful of jewels.*
Ezekiel 16:7b

*D*ear Beloved Believer,

In my next letter, I will begin to teach you about the breastplate of righteousness so that your heart may be protected from Lucifer's schemes. But before I do, I want to explain about some of the jewels that have been laid out before you. These jewels became rightfully yours the moment you accepted the King's offer of salvation, and it is important that you begin to adorn them each day. These jewels are priceless and should not be left lying around as if they were worthless.

Remember from the passages we examined in Ezekiel that when you were born, the cord tying you to the sin of Adam was not cut. But then the King passed by and said, "Live!" He chose you to be His child and clothed you in garments of salvation. After this miraculous event, the King Himself made you grow like a plant of the field. Look at what Ezekiel then says:

> You grew up and developed and became the most
> beautiful of jewels. Your breasts were formed and your
> hair grew, you who were naked and bare.
>
> —Ezekiel 16:7b

The King loves you so deeply that He desires you to grow and mature in Him. As you do, you will begin to draw closer and closer to Him, which will enable your relationship to be rich and fulfilling. One of the key elements to this growth is understanding the *righteousness*—a word that means "free from guilt or sin"[1]—that was accredited to you at the moment of your salvation. Listen to what Paul has to say:

> It is because of him that you are in Christ Jesus, who
> has become for us wisdom from God—that is, our
> righteousness, holiness and redemption.
>
> —1 Corinthians 1:30

According to the King's Word, there are two kinds of righteousness. The first is *imputed righteousness*, which is also known in layman terms as *positional righteousness*. Positional righteousness is *justification*, which means "just as if you had never sinned"! You received this precious jewel the moment you accepted the Prince of Peace as your Savior and Lord, and because of it, when the King in heaven now looks upon you, He sees you just as if you had never sinned! From the moment of your salvation, you became *positionally* righteous in Him.

The second form of righteousness is *imparted righteousness*, which is also known in layman terms as *practical righteousness*. Practical righteousness is *sanctification* or *holiness*, and it is the type of righteousness you live out in your daily walk with the King. From this, we see that righteousness is both a *one-time event* that occurred at the moment of your salvation and an *ongoing process* that you must live out on a daily basis.

Because of who you are in Christ, you have been set free from guilt and sin and are now able to walk in freedom. But again, because of love, there is a choice. You can choose to cherish the King's gift of freedom and wear this precious jewel in the secret place of your heart, or you can choose to leave it lying around. So, what will you choose to do with the righteousness the King has bestowed on you?

Now, each gem is priceless, but perhaps the one with the greatest value is the jewel of forgiveness. In Ephesians 1:7, Paul states, "In him we have redemption through his blood, the forgiveness of sins, in accordance with the riches of God's grace." Conceivably, "forgiveness" is one of the most beautiful words in the King's language, for it speaks of His deep love for you. Consider for a moment what Pastor Jon Courson has to say about the magnitude of this gift:

> Not a bone of Jesus was broken. Why is this a big deal? Because where is the blood continually produced in the body? It's produced in the bone. Therefore, [the King] mandated not a bone of His would be broken, ensuring a perpetual and inexhaustible supply of blood. That's why Paul could later declare, "Where sin abounds, grace abounds yet more." Truly, the blood of [the Prince of Peace] is sufficient to cleanse you from every sin you have ever committed or will commit. Why? Because not a bone of His was broken.[2]

As Paul notes, the King has "rescued us from the dominion of darkness and brought us into the kingdom of the Son he loves, in whom we have redemption, the forgiveness of sins" (Colossians 1:13-14). Because of this precious jewel, even though you stumble, fall and make mistakes, you can know that the Prince of Peace has already paid the price for your forgiveness. All you need to do to grasp this gem is confess your sins, and the King will forgive you and purify you from all unrighteousness. Never forget that He forgives *all* of your sins—past, present and future. Praise the Lord!

When you look more closely at the jewel of forgiveness, you will discover that it is of great purity and without flaw. As the King said, "I will cleanse you from all your impurities and from all your idols. I will give you a new heart and put a new spirit in you; I will remove from you your heart of stone and give you a heart of flesh" (Ezekiel 36:25-26). Notice the tense of the verbs in these verses—they are in the present tense, which means this is an *ongoing* washing and purifying of your sins. The King loves you so deeply that He takes your old heart of stone and gives you a new heart of flesh—a heart ready to receive His love—so He can meet with you in the secret place deep within your heart. The King also states in His Word:

> Come now, let us reason together. . . . Though your sins are like scarlet, they shall be as white as snow; though they are red as crimson, they shall be like wool.
> —Isaiah 1:18

Think of the beauty of the first winter's snow. It is so fresh, clean and pure. This is the gift that the King has given by bestowing the gem of forgiveness on you—you are fresh, clean and pure in His sight. You are washed clean because of who you are in Christ, the Prince of Peace.

But again, you have a choice. You can choose to accept this precious gem and wear it in the depths of your heart as you make wise choices based upon the King's forgiveness of your sin. Or you can choose to leave it lying around as if it is worthless. You do this every time you choose not to forgive yourself for your past mistakes and failures. What a shame! What a waste! Don't do this! Pick up this precious jewel and cherish it in the depths of your heart. Make wise decisions today based upon who you are in Christ—not who you use to be. As you do, you will be wearing this precious gem.

Another jewel the King has provided to you is *peace*, which you grasp by cherishing righteousness and forgiveness in the secret place of your heart. Sadly, many children of the King choose not to treasure this gift. They leave it lying around as they go about their daily lives in worry and fear—penniless—when they have this precious jewel available for their use. I want to encourage you to adorn this priceless jewel and walk in peace with your Prince, who is the Prince of Peace! In fact, the King Himself is known as Jehovah-Shalom, "the Lord Our Peace."

As Paul writes, "Since we have been *justified* [that's positional righteousness] through faith, we have *peace* with God through our Lord Jesus Christ" (Romans 5:1, emphasis added). It is as simple as that! Walk in wisdom, move your head knowledge of righteousness and forgiveness to your heart, accept the truth, believe it in your heart, and live your daily life according to this truth. Yes, I know that you are not worthy, but that is the beauty of these precious jewels the King has bestowed on you—they are *gifts* that have been given out of the deep love He has for you. You can't earn them.

As you cherish the precious jewels of righteousness, forgiveness, peace and justification deep within your heart, you will discover the most beautiful jewel of all: *your identity in Christ*, the Prince of Peace. Remember what the scribe Ezekiel said: "You grew up and developed and became the most beautiful of jewels" (Ezekiel 16:7b). You become the most beautiful of jewels the moment you start living your life based upon who you are in Christ and no longer upon your feelings and desires. That's why this jewel is one that is transparent and without flaw. It causes you to see clearly and examine yourself. It causes you to keep a short account with the King and admit your failings. It causes you to then accept His precious jewels of righteousness, forgiveness, peace and justification, because you realize the righteousness you have been given is not your own. It is a precious treasure to cherish.

As you cherish these precious jewels, you are being transformed into the Prince of Peace's likeness to reflect His glory. But remember, this is not because of anything you have done—it is all because of who you are in Christ! But I must warn you: Lucifer, your archenemy, will try to confuse you by saying that your worth is in and of itself—that your righteousness is your own. However, as Paul notes, "As it is written: 'None is righteous, no, not one. . . no one does good, not even one'" (Romans 3:10,12b, ESV). On your own, you are nothing.

Many mighty men of the King knew this to be true. John the Baptist said, "After me will come one more powerful than I, the thongs of whose sandals I am not worthy to stoop down and untie" (Mark 1:7). He was speaking of the coming of the King's Son, the Prince of Peace. But perhaps the apostle Paul said it best: "I know *nothing good lives in me*, that is, in my sinful nature. For I have the desire to do what is good, but I cannot carry it out. . . . What a wretched man I am!" (Romans 7:18,24a, emphasis added).

Lucifer, the schemer, likes to spread the lie of *self-esteem*. He gets the world to sell this lie every day by bombarding you with advertisements that claim you need this or that to "feel better about yourself." Your flesh will naturally desire to buy this lie, as there will be times when you will feel worthless. So you must be prepared. Listen to what Luke, one of the King's scribes, wrote concerning self-esteem:

> To some who were confident of their own righteous-
> ness and looked down on everybody else, Jesus told

this parable: "Two men went up to the temple to pray, one a Pharisee and the other a tax collector. The Pharisee stood up and prayed about himself: 'God, I thank you that I am not like other men—robbers, evildoers, adulterers—or even like this tax collector. I fast twice a week and give a tenth of all I get.' But the tax collector stood at a distance. He would not even look up to heaven, but beat his breast and said, 'God, have mercy on me, a sinner.' I tell you that this man, rather than the other, *went home justified before God.* For everyone who *exalts himself* will be *humbled*, and he who *humbles himself* will be *exalted*."

—Luke 18:9-14, emphasis added

The King adorned the tax collector in clothes of righteousness, forgave his sins, and credited him with righteousness—not his own, but that which comes from the Prince of Peace. There are many well-meaning children of the King who are confused about this issue, so do not get caught up in this lie. Listen to what Pastor Bob Hoekstra has to say: "Esteem means to hold in high regard. Self-esteem [then, is] learning to hold yourself in high regard."[3] This is just a politically correct word for pride! See how Lucifer has twisted words once again?

There are so many verses in the King's Word that speak of the evil of pride. You are warned that pride goes before destruction (see Proverbs 16:18). When you are filled with pride, you do not seek the King (see Psalm 10:4). Your pride will only breed quarrels (see Proverbs 13:10). And, as Proverbs 11:2 clearly states, "When pride comes, then comes disgrace." I am sure that you do not want any more disgrace in your life! So discover the truth. The King's Word states, "There is a way that seems right to a man, but in the end it leads to death" (Proverbs 14:12; 16:25). Walk in this way that leads to life—

the King's way, not the world's way! Humble yourself to the will of the King, for He has great plans for you.

There will be times when you will feel down and blue. This is a normal part of life. Many times, the King will allow you to feel this way because you have walked away from His presence or away from the plans He has for you. This is when you need to kneel at the foot of the cross and ask the King to reveal if you have made a wrong turn. Give the King permission to search you. Cry out like the King's scribe David did when he wrote, "Search me, O God, and know my heart; test me and know my anxious thoughts. See if there is any offensive way in me, and lead me in the way everlasting" (Psalm 139:23-24).

Oftentimes, this down-and-blue feeling will be the conviction of the Holy Spirit, the Royal Counselor, leading you to repentance. He wants to lead you back to a right relationship with the King, so do not fall into Lucifer's trap by trying to raise your self-esteem. Instead, fall to your knees, allow the King to sprinkle clean water on you, and realize it is Christ-esteem that you need to learn more about and cherish in your life. Remember that if you confess your sins, He is faithful and just and will forgive you and purify you from all unrighteousness.

In view of what you have learned, always cherish and treasure the fact that you are the righteousness of the King. Let pure water wash over you as you embrace it: *"I am the righteousness of the King."*

Know that you are fully forgiven from all your sins—past, present and future—and washed clean. Accept the pardon and let the truth wash over you as you embrace it: *"I am forgiven and washed clean."*

Because of the precious jewels of righteousness and forgiveness, you are at peace with the King. Cherish it in the secret place of your heart: *"I am at peace with the King."*

Remember that the King looks on you and sees you just as if you had never sinned. Claim it by the King's authority: *"I am justified."*

You are created in the King's image to reflect His glory. So allow Him to shine forth as you come to understand, *"I am created in the King's image to reflect His glory."*

Adorn all of these precious jewels, in the depths of your heart, as you make decisions based upon who you are in the King's Son, Jesus Christ. As you do, shout it out for all to hear, *"I am able to walk in freedom."*

As promised, in my next letter I will give you vital information on the breastplate of righteousness. This important piece of the King's armor will enable you to safeguard the secret place where your precious jewels are stored and cherished. Until that time, never forget that you are the most beautiful of jewels.

Reflecting Him,
Your Faithful Servant of the King

Chapter Ten

Adorned in the Breastplate of Righteousness

You Are Free from Condemnation

But since we belong to the day, let us be self-controlled,
putting on faith and love as a breastplate.
1 Thessalonians 5:8a

$\mathcal{D}$ear Beloved Believer,

With the knowledge you gained in my last letter, you are now prepared to "put on the breastplate of righteousness" (Ephesians 6:14, NKJV). This is perhaps the most essential piece in the King's armor, as it covers a vital organ—an organ that is the wellspring of life—your heart. It was with your heart that you believed and were justified. It is with your heart that you turn head knowledge into life-changing heart knowledge so you can walk in wisdom. And it is deep within your heart in the secret place that you have a real, intimate, personal relationship with your Prince of Peace.

Previously, I told you that when Paul wrote the book of Ephesians, he was being held in a Roman prison. With this in mind, let's learn about the importance of the breastplate to the Roman soldiers of Paul's day. As Pastor Warren Wiersbe explains, "[The breastplate] was a coat of mail that covered the front and the back of the soldier's body from the neck to the thighs."[1] This piece was a "fishscale-like construction of small metal plates sewn to cloth or leather. . . . The scales could number as high as 700-1000 per 'coat.' Each coat obviously could be quite heavy and expensive to produce."[2] This is true of your breastplate as well, for it was purchased by the blood of the King's own Son, the Prince of Peace.

The breastplate, which was attached to the Roman soldier's belt to hold it securely in place, was used to protect the soldier from the enemy's superb archers and their fiery darts. In the same way, you must remain in the King's Word and gird "your waist with truth" (Ephesians 6:14b, NKJV) each day so that your breastplate will be securely fastened in place. If you don't secure it, you will be exposed and vulnerable to "all the fiery darts of the wicked one" (Ephesians 6:16b, NKJV). This is why it is important to believe, understand and cherish *who you are in Christ.* When you come to realize the truth of your identity in Christ, *and make decisions based upon that truth*, you will be using your breastplate of righteousness in the way the King designed it to be used.

Like the Roman soldier's breastplate, the breastplate of righteousness is constructed with a number of small metal plates or shields. Because of the King's great love for you, each is engraved with the truth of *who you are in Christ*— various "I am" statements. Can you see it? Each of these small, metal shields is inscribed with a true statement about you: "I am loved," "I am someone special," "I am not a mistake," "I am saved," "I am a child of the King," "I am the bride of Christ," "I am justified." These true statements completely adorn your breastplate of righteousness. Better yet, each statement has been engraved with nail-scarred hands and, in love, sewn into place to protect your heart.

The breastplate is the truth of the Word that states you are washed clean and made righteous. The Prince of Peace

Himself has placed this breastplate on you so that you can stand justified before the King, who is also known as Jehovah-Tsidkenu, "the Lord Our Righteousness." While you, on your own, could never be good enough to receive righteousness, you can never be bad enough to lose it. Praise the Lord!

Of course, Lucifer, the traitor, will try to convince you that this is not true and that this piece of armor can be taken from you. He will use four strategies to try to condemn you: (1) accuse you directly, (2) get you to accuse yourself, (3) get others to accuse you, and (4) attempt to show you that the circumstances accuse you. However, by effectively adorning the breastplate of righteousness, you can overcome these attacks. So take heart, for you are not fighting *for* victory but *from* victory—the Prince of Peace has already defeated Satan. You already know the end of the story:

> Then I heard a loud voice in heaven say: "Now have come the salvation and the power and the kingdom of our God, and the authority of his Christ. For the accuser of our brothers, who accuses them before our God day and night, has been hurled down."
> —Revelation 12:10

When Lucifer accuses you *directly*—his first strategy—he does so before the throne of the King. It's interesting that when he talks to you about the King, he lies and twists the Word; but when he talks to the King about you, he usually tells the truth. It is absolutely true that you have made mistakes and sinned—and that you will make many more mistakes in the future. You are just like the King's scribe, the apostle Paul, who wrote, "Wretched man that I am!" (Romans 7:24a, NKJV). But the moment you take these sins to the foot of the cross and confess them to the King, He purifies you from all unrighteousness and restores your relationship. Therefore, understand that when Lucifer is shooting fiery darts, he is aiming at your heart—at the heart of your relationship with the King. This is all the more reason why you must stand firm with your breastplate securely covering your heart.

It's important to know that if you choose *not* to believe the truth of who you are in Christ, you leave your breastplate lying around, and it will be useless to you. For this reason, move the truth of the King's Word—that you are free from condemnation and purified from all unrighteousness—from your head to your heart. You do this in a practical manner every time you make wise decisions based not upon your feelings and desires but upon the truth of who you are in Christ. As you do this, you will be adorning the breastplate of righteousness in the manner the King intended.

Lucifer's second strategy is to set you up to *accuse yourself*. He lies in wait like a prowling lion, ready to pounce when he sees an opportunity. Sadly, many of the King's children have fallen victim to this tactic and have been rendered ineffective because they focus only on their past mistakes and sins. I have known many who have even considered suicide as a means to end both Lucifer's accusations and their own. But this is not in the King's plans! The Prince of Peace placed the breastplate of righteousness on you at the moment of salvation and *positioned* it to protect your heart. You must choose to wear it each day by accepting the truth of who you are in Christ.

The way to counteract Lucifer's fiery darts of accusation is to refuse to focus on your past mistakes and sins—for the truth is that you *are* a wretched sinner—and simply agree, "Yes, I am a wretched sinner." Then, instead of allowing these words to condemn you, use them as a reminder of where you came from! Know deep in your heart, in the innermost secret place, that because of the King's love, you are a new creation in Christ. Then just admit the truth: "I am a wretched sinner, but, praise the Lord, I am forgiven, washed clean and am a new creation in Christ!"

When it seems that all you are thinking about is your past failures, you must focus on the truth of the Word and move forward. As Paul writes, "One thing I do: forgetting what lies behind and straining forward to what lies ahead, I press on toward the goal for the prize of the upward call of God in Christ Jesus" (Philippians 3:13b-14, ESV). Recognize that while you cannot change the past, you can change the future, and *press on toward the goal.*

This brings us to Lucifer's third tactic: getting *others* to accuse you. Have you ever noticed that almost everyone the King used mightily in His Word was falsely accused at one point or another? David was falsely accused over and over again. Throughout the psalms, you will find that he prayed and asked the King to silence his enemies who told lies about him. The apostle Paul was also falsely accused many times and thrown into prison. Yet look at the weapons he used to strengthen himself: "By truthful speech, and the power of God; with the weapons of righteousness for the right hand and for the left" (2 Corinthians 6:7, ESV).

Even the King's own Son, the Prince of Peace, was falsely accused. Lucifer used others to accuse Him of being addicted to wine (see Matthew 11:10). He was labeled as being demon-possessed (see John 7:20). He was even falsely accused and condemned to death on the charges of being a blasphemer (see Matthew 26:65). Given this, you can be certain that if the Prince of Peace was falsely accused, at some point in your walk with the King you will also be falsely accused.

But do not despair or lose hope. When the fiery darts turn into fiery words of accusation, make sure the breastplate of righteousness is securely fastened to your belt of truth. If you remember and choose to believe the truth about your *identity in Christ*, your heart will be covered, and you will be able to stand firm from a point of strength and confidence. If you have the breastplate in place, the enemy will not be able to penetrate your heart with the deceptive accusations he gets others to throw at you.

The final strategy that Lucifer will use to accuse you is to get you to believe that the *circumstances and difficulties you are facing* are a result of something you have done. He will try to get you to believe this lie by saying the King is allowing you to suffer as a form of punishment for your sins. Of course, this is preposterous, because the King loves you deeply and does not punish you. At times He may *discipline* you, but this discipline speaks of His love. Let's look at this distinction a bit more closely.

The purpose of enacting a *punishment* is to inflict a penalty for wrongdoing.[3] The purpose of *discipline*, on the other hand, is to teach, train, correct or mold to perfect a person's moral character.[4] Can you see the love contained within discipline? The King desires to *mold you* and *shape you* into the person He created you to be. You are His work of art, and you have been created to do a good work. While the wrong choices you make will cause you to experience difficulties because there are consequences to sin, the King will not use those consequences as punishment. Instead, He will use them as a refining process to mold, shape and perfect your moral character as you grow and mature in His ways.

This was certainly true in Job's case. The Word states that the King had blessed Job for his perseverance, yet Job was still allowed to endure terrible difficulties. Lucifer was not only given permission to strike at Job's family and destroy everything he had, but he was even given permission to strike at Job's health and afflict him with painful sores. Why did the King allow all this to happen? He did so in order to refine Job and mold him. Lucifer had claimed, "Stretch out your hand and strike everything he has, and he will surely curse you to your face" (Job 1:11), but the King knew that Job would pass the test.

At one point, Job's friends tried to convince him that his affliction was a punishment from the King for some sin he had committed. In view of this, understand that Lucifer will sometimes use other children of the King—and sometimes even the King's teachers—to make you believe your difficulties are a result of some unconfessed sin. Lucifer loves to twist the King's Word and cause confusion, which is why it is important to take the Word in full context. Let me share an example.

One day, the Prince of Peace and His disciples were walking along when they encountered a blind man. The disciples asked Him, "Rabbi, who sinned, this man or his parents, that he was born blind?" (John 9:2). Listen carefully to the answer the Prince of Peace gave: "Neither this man nor his parents sinned . . . but this happened so that the work of God might be displayed in his life" (John 9:3). The King will allow suffering to refine you and draw you closer to Him because He desires to have a real, intimate, personal relationship with you. And as you draw closer to Him during difficulties, you will be able to glorify Him in *all* things and be the witness He calls you to be.

But remember that once again you have a choice. You can choose to draw closer to the King through these rough times, or you can choose to believe the lies of Lucifer and pull away from Him. If you stand firm in the midst of difficulties, your life will serve as an example to others. As the Prince of Peace has said, "You are the light of the world.

A city set on a hill cannot be hidden. . . . Let your light shine before others, so that they may see your good works and give glory to your Father who is in heaven (Matthew 5:14,16, ESV).

Lucifer, the traitor, wants to destroy your light. He wants to take away your witness as a believer in the one and only true King. To achieve this goal, he will torment you by reminding you of all your past mistakes and sins. He wants to make you feel unworthy to serve the King, but don't let him succeed. Do not focus on yourself or your sins (and carelessly lay aside your breastplate), for this will only lead to defeat and despair. Instead, keep your breastplate of righteousness firmly in place as you admit the truth: *"I am a wretched sinner."*

But that is as far as it goes! When the accusations begin, instead of engaging in a pity party, rejoice in the truth of your identity in the Prince of Peace. Say it boldly—*"I am a new creation in Christ"*—for the old has passed away and the new has come!

When Lucifer condemns you, remember that you are free from his accusations. Cheer it out loud for all to hear of your freedom—*"I am free from condemnation"*—for your Advocate, the Prince of Peace, is standing at the right hand of the King, at this very moment, interceding for you.

While you are at it, remember that you are purified from all unrighteousness. Shout it out loud, *"I am purified from all unrighteousness!"*

Lucifer, your adversary, will have others falsely accuse you, but no one can separate you from the King's love. Therefore, be encouraged that the circumstances and difficulties you are facing will refine you. The King has not given these circumstances to punish you, no matter what Lucifer wants you to believe, but to mold you, for you are the King's work of art. Move this truth from your head to your heart as you say, *"I am His work of art created to do good works."*

You are the light of the world. State it with authority: *"I am the light of the world."* For this reason, you are able to always walk in the Light. Shine brightly as you move forward and say, *"I am able to walk in the Light."*

Until the time I can write more concerning fiery trials, adorn your breastplate of righteousness and by faith believe the truth of the Word. Hold fast to every piece of truth, for if you allow even one hole to appear in your breastplate, Lucifer will aim for it. Hold fast to the truth of *who you are in Christ* so that your breastplate will be complete and your heart relationship with the King will be protected.

Adorned in the breastplate,
Your Willing Servant

Chapter Eleven

Covered by the King's Garment

You Are Redeemed

*And we, who with unveiled faces
all reflect the Lord's glory,
are being transformed into his likeness
with ever-increasing glory.*
2 Corinthians 3:18

$\mathcal{D}$ear Beloved Believer,

Have you ever marveled at the look of love between a bridegroom and his bride the moment the veil is removed? Have you seen their eyes sparkle at that first moment when they are face to face? And what about the moment when the person officiating the ceremony declares, "I now pronounce you man and wife. You may kiss the bride!" Although the happy couple is in a room full of people, it is as if all others vanish. They have eyes only for each other.

Well, I want to tell you that there is a love much deeper awaiting you that can only be discovered as you draw closer to your Bridegroom, the Prince of Peace. For this reason, I am going to share a story—a wonderful story—that reflects the love your Prince has for you. This true account took place, according to the King's Word, during a time when "there was no king in Israel [and] everyone did what was right in his own eyes" (Judges 17:6, NKJV). I imagine it was much like today, where most people choose not to follow the King and also do what is right in their own eyes.

It all began when there was a severe famine in the land of Israel and a man from Bethlehem, together with his wife and two sons, went to live in the country of Moab. While the family was there, the man died and left his wife, Naomi, a widow. Both of Naomi's sons married Moabite women; and after a time, they also died, leaving her destitute and her daughters-in-law also widows. Then one day word came to Naomi that the famine in Israel was over. So Naomi and her two daughters-in-law prepared to return there.

Now, it is important to understand that the Moabites were bitter enemies of the Israelites. So, out of love and concern for her daughters-in-law, Naomi urged them to return to their mothers' homes and remain in Moab. One of the women chose to stay with her own people, but the other woman, who was named Ruth, refused! She pleaded with Naomi from the depth of her heart and said:

> Don't urge me to leave you or to turn back from you. Where you go I will go, and where you stay I will stay. Your people will be my people and your God my God.
>
> —Ruth 1:16

So Naomi and Ruth traveled to Bethlehem and arrived at the start of the barley harvest. They were poor and had no way to survive on their own. Ruth, out of love for Naomi, said, "Let me go to the fields and pick up the leftover grain behind anyone in whose eyes I find favor" (Ruth 2:2). At the time, there was a law of Moses (known as the law of gleaning) that instructed landowners to make only one pass through the fields while harvesting. Any produce the harvesters missed would be left for the poor and widowed so they could glean for their own needs. So, as the King's Word tells us, Ruth "went out and began to glean in the fields be-hind the harvesters" (Ruth 2:3a).

Ruth's actions show that she loved Naomi deeply, be-cause by going to the fields to glean she was possibly put-ting herself in harm's way. Think about it—she was a young woman who was not only poor but also of a nationality that is a bitter enemy of the Israelites. She had no way to pro-tect herself if someone decided to take advantage of her. But the King loved Ruth, and He desired to provide for her *and* protect her. So, unknown to her, He sent someone to watch over her.

As it turned out, Ruth "found herself working in a field belonging to Boaz" (Ruth 2:3b). Boaz was a relative of her father-in-law. If you look at the events of this story closely, you will discover that the King was divinely orchestrating the events in Ruth's life. Remember that she had given up everything when she chose to follow Naomi. She had said, "Your people will be my people *and your God my God*" (Ruth 1:16, emphasis added). Ruth chose to forsake everything to choose to follow the one and only true King. As a result, she discovered the depth of the King's love, for Boaz was a kinsman-redeemer.

To understand the role of a "kinsman-redeemer," I must explain two additional laws in the land of Israel. One was the law of *redemption*. If an Israelite sold some of his prop-erty and was later unable to repurchase it, his nearest relative could come and redeem what his family member had sold. This law protected Israel, kept the property in the original family, and continued the family's name. In simpler terms, when a piece of property was sold, it was more like a lease. At the end of the lease, the original owner would repurchase or redeem the property. If the original owner was unable to do so because he had died or could not afford it, then a family member had first choice to redeem it. This relative was known as the "kinsman-redeemer."

The second law (which, unknown to Ruth, was about to change her life) was the law of the *levirate* (also known as the *levirate marriage*). According to the King's Word, this law said:

> If brothers are living together and one of them dies without a son, his widow must not marry outside the family. Her husband's brother shall take her and marry her and fulfill the duty of a brother-in-law to her. The first son she bears shall carry on the name of the dead brother so that his name will not be blotted out from Israel.
>
> —Deuteronomy 25:5-6

In other words, if a man died without an heir, his brother was to marry the grieving widow. If the man did not have a brother, the next nearest living male relative (known as the kinsman-redeemer) was to fulfill the role. Under this law, a widow who did not have a son could go to her husband's nearest relative and ask him to marry her in order to provide an heir for her deceased husband.

There were three conditions required to fulfill the levirate marriage. First, the man had to be related as a kinsman-redeemer to the man who had died. Second, he had to be available for marriage. Third, he had to be willing. The law did not *require* the kinsman to accept this role; however, if he chose not to accept the widow's hand in marriage, he had to remove one of his sandals as a symbol of shame. From then on, his family would be known as "the family of the unsandled." Although this does not sound like a symbol of shame to our way of thinking, in their culture it was serious! This action signified that the kinsman was *walking away* from his responsibility.

So it was that the King directed Ruth to the field of Boaz. One day while she was out in the field following the harvesters and gleaning from the leftover grain, "Boaz arrived from Bethlehem and greeted the harvesters, 'The LORD be with you!'" (Ruth 2:4a). Boaz was a godly man who was highly respected and had a kind spirit. Even though most chose to do what was right in their own eyes, Boaz chose to follow the one and only true King. Because of this, the King was about to bless him, for Ruth immediately caught his eye. Boaz asked his foreman, "Whose young woman is that?" (Ruth 2:5). It is as if you can almost hear him say, "Wow!"

The foreman explained that she was the woman who came back from Moab with Naomi and that she had asked to glean behind the harvesters. He went on to explain how hard Ruth had worked during the morning hours. Well, this really caught Boaz's attention, for he soon approached her and said:

> My daughter, listen to me. Don't go and glean in another field and don't go away from here. Stay here with my servant girls. Watch the field where the men are harvesting, and follow along after the girls. I have told the men not to touch you. And whenever you are thirsty, go and get a drink from the water jars the men have filled.
>
> —Ruth 2:8-9

Notice that Boaz *immediately began to provide for Ruth.* Do not overlook this, for it is an important aspect of the story. Boaz told his men not to touch her, and he also asked her not to harvest in another's field. Why? Because he could not protect her there!

In the same way, our King provides for us and protects us. In fact, He is also known as Jehovah-Jireh, "the Lord Will Provide," and Jehovah-Nissi, "the Lord Our Banner of

Protection." Many times when He is orchestrating events to provide for us and protect us, we are not even aware of the fact. We may even run the other way or go into a field where the King doesn't want us to go. We take so much for granted.

In amazement of Boaz's favor, Ruth bowed before him and asked, "Why have I found such favor in your eyes that you notice me—a foreigner?" (Ruth 2:10b). Was she about to say "a Moabitess," "an enemy," or any of the other derogatory remarks she had probably heard mentioned about her people? She certainly must have felt unworthy of his favor and astonished at the grace he was bestowing upon her. She knew it was undeserved, yet she accepted it in reverence as she bowed face down before him.

We can learn a lot from this woman. As Pastor Wiersbe explains, "[Ruth] acknowledged her own unworthiness and accepted [Boaz's] grace. She believed his promises and rejoiced in them. . . . Ruth neither looked back at her tragic past nor did she look at herself and consider her sorry plight. She fell at the feet of the master and submitted herself to him. She looked away from her poverty and focused on his riches. She forgot her fears and rested on his promises."[1]

We also need to acknowledge our unworthiness and accept the King's grace. We need to believe His promises and rejoice in them. We need to forget our past failings and look forward to the future. We need to fall to His feet in reverence and submit our lives to Him. We need to forget our lack and focus on His unsearchable riches—riches that He has already bestowed on us.

Boaz already knew of Ruth's struggles. There had been talk in the small town of Bethlehem, and he knew she had forsaken all to follow the one and only true King. Listen to how he replied to her question as to why she had found favor in his eyes:

I've been told all about what you have done for your mother-in-law since the death of your husband—how you left your father and mother and your homeland and came to live with a people you did not know before. May the LORD repay you for what you have done. May you be richly rewarded by the LORD, the God of Israel, under whose wings you have come to take refuge.

—Ruth 2:11-12

Just as Boaz knew of Ruth and her difficulties, the King knows of you and your struggles. He knows you gave up all to follow Him. He knows that many around you do not understand the commitment you have made. But do not give up hope. Continue to walk in faith as Ruth did, for the King of kings will provide for you and protect you, just as He provided for and protected Ruth. The King loves you more than you know!

As this love story continues, Boaz told his men to pull out some barley stalks and leave them for Ruth to pick up. When she came home that evening, Naomi saw the over-abundance of grain and realized that something amazing was happening. You can almost hear the wonder in her voice as she asked Ruth, "Where did you glean today? Where did you work? Blessed be the man who took notice of you!" (Ruth 2:19b). When Ruth explained that she had worked in Boaz's field, you can almost see the wheels turning in Naomi's mind. Her motherly instincts and matchmaking abilities switched on, and she said, "That man is our close relative; he is one of our kinsman-redeemers" (Ruth 2:20b).

When the harvest was finished and the work almost complete, Naomi took action. She said to Ruth, "My daughter, should I not try to find a home for you, where you will be well provided for? Is not Boaz . . . a kinsman of ours? Tonight he will be winnowing barley on the threshing floor. Wash and

101

perfume yourself, and put on your best clothes. . . . When he lies down, note the place where he is lying. Then go and uncover his feet and lie down. He will tell you what to do" (Ruth 3:1-4). Ruth did as Naomi instructed and lay down at Boaz's feet. In the night, something startled Boaz, and he awakened to find Ruth there. When he asked who she was, Ruth replied, "I am your servant Ruth. . . . Spread the corner of your garment over me, since you are a kinsman-redeemer" (Ruth 3:9).

Although Naomi's instructions to Ruth may appear a bit forward, her aim in having Ruth lay at Boaz's feet was to appeal to his kinsman obligation to take her as his wife.[2] In simpler terms, Ruth was applying the law of the levirate marriage and asking Boaz to marry her. We can see that Boaz did not take her actions as being forward or interpret them as something different, for he said to her, "All my fellow townsmen know that you are a woman of noble character" (Ruth 3:11b).

Boaz certainly did have an interest in Ruth and wanted to be her kinsman-redeemer, but as the story unfolds we learn that there was a relative closer in line than him. So, the next day, Boaz went to the city gates and spoke to this man. For reasons unknown, this man was not willing to redeem the estate because it would "endanger [his] own estate" (Ruth 4:6a). So he removed his sandal. Although this was a sign of humiliation, to Boaz it was a license for marriage! He was able to act in love as Ruth's kinsman-redeemer.

The King impressed upon my heart to share this beautiful love story with you because the symbolism of Boaz spreading the corner of his garment over Ruth is an amazing picture of the love the King has for you. This was a statement that he would marry her. It was a binding action, much like a written contract today. (In fact, it is still practiced in some parts of the Middle East.³) In this way, Boaz represents your Kinsman Redeemer, and Ruth represents you, the bride of Christ.

But there is even more to discover concerning this act. Does "the corner of my garment" remind you of anything? Remember the words of love spoken through the prophet Ezekiel:

> Later I passed by, and when I looked at you and saw that you were old enough for love, I spread *the corner of my garment* over you and covered your nakedness. I gave you my solemn oath and *entered into a covenant with you*, declares the Sovereign LORD, and *you became mine.*
>
> —Ezekiel 16:8, emphasis added

Although Ezekiel wrote these verses to the Jewish nation of Israel as an allegory of Jerusalem, they parallel your own walk with the King. From the moment of your salvation, you entered into a covenant with the Prince of Peace and became His bride. He says in His Word, "I am my beloved's, and my beloved is mine" (Song of Songs 6:3a, NKJV). This describes you! You will discover this scarlet thread woven from the beginning to the end of the Word. Every book, every story and every theme from Genesis to Revelation points to this scarlet thread—the scarlet thread of *redemption*. For you have been redeemed from the hand of Lucifer, the enemy!

The word "redeemed" means "to buy back; to win back; to free from what distresses or harms; to free from captivity by payment of ransom; to free from the consequences of sin; to change for the better; to convert into something of value and to atone for."⁴ All these are true of you! Your Kinsman Redeemer spread the corner of His garment over you to buy you back from Lucifer, the thief. Your Kinsman Redeemer desires to free you from that which will cause you harm. In fact, He freed you from captivity by payment of a ransom. "Paid in full" was written in blood to free you from the penalty of sin. Because of the deep love He has for you, He desires to change you for the better—to redeem you and convert you into something of value.

Previously, I told you that before the Prince of Peace came into the world, there were 613 different decrees the King required to be kept.[5] Those who could not meet these decrees were guilty of committing sin. But there was a blessing contained within the Law, for it points us to the King's Son, the Prince of Peace, our Kinsman Redeemer. He is the only One who can set us free from the penalty of sin. As Pastor Jon Courson writes, "The more you read the Law, study the Law, and know the Law—the more you realize that the Law is not your redeemer. It's your condemner. The Law points out your weaknesses, your failings, and your flaws."[6]

In view of this truth, always remember this precious gift of redemption, and never be so foolish as to try to reach the goal by human effort. For the Word declares, "Clearly no one is justified before God by the law" (Galatians 3:11). Always hold fast to the gift and allow the fact that you have been redeemed to change you for the better—to change you into something of worth. You were redeemed from the curse of the Law.

Paul, the King's scribe, wrote, "All who rely on observing the law are under a curse, for it is written: 'Cursed is everyone who does not continue to do everything written in the Book of the Law'" (Galatians 3:10). I pray that if you have been trying to live your life as a "good person," you now realize it is an absolute impossibility. All who try have a veil that covers their heart. But the Prince of Peace, your Bridegroom, can lift this veil. Listen to these beautiful words penned in love:

> Whenever anyone turns to the Lord, *the veil is taken away*. . . . And we, who with *unveiled faces all reflect the Lord's glory*, are being transformed into his likeness with ever-increasing glory.
>
> —2 Corinthians 3:16-18a, emphasis added

When your Bridegroom paid the price for your sins on the cross, the veil in the Temple that separated the place where the King dwelt (known as the Holy of Holies) from humanity was torn in two (see Matthew 27:51). Your Bridegroom removed this veil in love so He could meet with you in the secret place and look upon you—face to face. Remember the look of love I described at the beginning of this letter—the look that passes between the bride and bridegroom when the veil is taken away? That same look occurs when your Kinsman Redeemer removes the veil that has covered your heart.

As you look to your Kinsman Redeemer in the secret place and He looks on you, His love and His glory come shining down upon your face and are reflected to those around you. *This is yet another reason why you were given life: to glorify Him!* And as you meet with Him daily, you are transformed into His likeness. This is *practical righteousness*—the righteousness that is lived out in your daily walk with your Prince. As you grow and mature in the way of the King, you are transformed into His Son's likeness with ever-increasing glory.

Now that the veil has been removed, never forget to look into your Bridegroom's eyes, for there you will see how wide and long and high and deep is the love He has for you (see Ephesians 3:18). Wait for my next letters, for within them I will show how you can continue to be transformed into His likeness and reflect His glory. Until that time, remember that you are redeemed. Shout it out in love: *"I am redeemed!"*

Never return to the yoke of the Law. For you know the truth: *"I am redeemed from the curse of the Law."*

In view of this, walk in faith as Ruth walked. Gain courage as you believe in your heart, *"I am able to walk in faith."*

Remember that the King loves and cares for you so deeply that He has redeemed you out of the hand of Lucifer, the enemy. Let Him hear you say it: *"I am redeemed from the hand of the enemy."*

Bask in the King's love, His provision and His protection as you are transformed into His likeness. For you are covered by His garment. Let it wrap around your heart as you whisper it in awe, *"I am covered by the corner of His garment."*

Reminisce about the day the veil was removed and look to Him, face to face, so you can reflect His glory. Remember that this is one of the reasons why you were given life!

Reflecting His glory,
Your Fellow Harvester

Chapter Twelve

Free from Filthy Rags

You Are Washed Clean

All of us have become like one who is unclean,
and all our righteous acts are like filthy rags.
Isaiah 64:6

*D*ear Beloved Believer,

Because one of the reasons why you were given life is to reflect the King's glory, it is time to walk worthy of your calling. Do you have a peace that surpasses understanding? Or do you struggle with strongholds such as depression, anxiety, rage and/or self-destructive behaviors? In my last letter, I told you about the King's garment, which He has spread over you to cover your nakedness. In this letter, I want to show you that no one has the right to uncover that which the King has covered. This is critical for you to know, because Lucifer will use the wrongful uncovering as a means to set up strongholds in your life. Look once again at the verses in Ezekiel, which are rich with meaning:

> You grew up and developed and became the most beautiful of jewels. Your breasts were formed and your hair grew, you who were naked and bare. Later I passed by, and when I looked at you and saw that you were old enough for love, I spread the corner of my garment over you and covered your nakedness. I gave

107

you my solemn oath and entered into a covenant with you, declares the Sovereign LORD, and you became mine. I bathed you with water and washed the blood from you and put ointments on you.

—Ezekiel 16:7-9

These verses describe a bride as she matures and develops physically. The blood referred to in this passage is most likely menstrual blood.[1] Given this, we see that when the King saw that the bride was *old enough for love*—physical love—He spread the corner of His garment over her to protect her from harm. As you learned in the last letter, when the King said, "I spread the corner of my garment over you," it was symbolic of entering into a marriage contract. The King created the physical union between a man and a woman for the specific purpose of uniting them as one. But this beautiful, physical relationship is reserved *only* for marriage.

Let's look back at the first wedding in history. As we read in the King's Word, "The LORD God made a woman from the rib he had taken out of the man, and *he brought her to the man*" (Genesis 2:22, emphasis added). Out of His deep love, the King, God the Father, gave Eve to Adam, just as He gave you to be the bride of His Son, the Prince of Peace. Listen to how the King's Word describes the event:

The man said, "This is now bone of my bones and flesh of my flesh; she shall be called 'woman,' for she was taken out of man." For this reason a man will leave his father and mother and be united to his wife, and they will become one flesh. The man and his wife were both naked, and they felt no shame.

—Genesis 2:23-25

Notice that the man and wife were both naked, yet felt no shame. When you are in the King's perfect will, there is no shame; but the moment you step out of His will, there is both shame and consequences. This is because the King loves you deeply and knows what will hurt you. He created the physical union between a man and a woman specifically for marriage. He created this union to be beautiful, to be pleasurable, to bring intimacy within the marriage, and to be a special relationship set apart from all other relationships. It's important to know that everything the King made was beautiful, but many times Lucifer, the serpent, will twist and destroy it, for he comes only to steal, kill and destroy (see John 10:10).

This is exactly what the enemy has done with sexual immorality. In fact, the word "immorality" has almost fallen out of usage. Today, the world believes and sells the lie that sex outside of marriage is perfectly acceptable. If something feels good, it is perfectly fine to do it. But I, dearly beloved, am a living testimony that this is not true. When I was young I believed the lies of the enemy, and his lies almost destroyed me. The King calls you to be holy, and there are consequences to sin! There is no getting around that fact. Listen to His warning of love written down by Paul:

> It is God's will that you should be sanctified: that you should avoid sexual immorality; that each of you should learn to control his own body in a way that is holy and honorable, not in passionate lust like the heathen, who do not know God.
>
> —1 Thessalonians 4:3-5

The King did not make this decree to cause your life to be empty and hollow but to give you hope and fulfillment. He loves you deeply and desires to protect you in love. He knows that sexual immorality will hurt you, and that if you choose to live in this lifestyle, it will eventually destroy you.

Your relationship with the Groom, the Prince of Peace, is to be like the relationship between a husband and wife.

You are called into intimate fellowship with Him. There is a special place, a private place, where the husband and wife seek a deeper intimacy with each other—a place where they have a special relationship set apart from all other relationships—and the Prince desires to have this kind of special relationship with you. He desires to meet with you in the secret place where true love and intimacy can be expressed.

Now, please do not misunderstand me. I am not speaking about some twisted relationship, but about *true intimacy*. I am speaking about knowing one another deep within your heart, in the secret place, within the boundaries of your marriage to the Prince of Peace. This relationship is an intimacy of the heart, for He is the only one who truly knows you. He knows your hurts and your failures. He knows your hopes and your dreams. He knows *everything* about you.

This is why the King commanded you to be set apart. This is why He desires you not to be sexually active outside of marriage. He knows that wrong relationships will hurt and confuse you. He knows that they will cause you to *not* fully understand the deep intimacy of the heart that takes place within the boundaries of marriage between one man and one woman for life. If you choose to enter into a relationship outside of this design, it will weaken your understanding of the true intimacy that the Prince of Peace desires to have with you. This is why the King's Word declares:

> But in your hearts set apart Christ as Lord.
> —1 Peter 3:15a

Lucifer knows this truth, and he wants to twist your thinking. Remember, he is the author of confusion and the father of all lies. He wants you to be hurt over and over again in wrong relationships so that you will hoard and stuff all the pain deep inside your heart. Lucifer knows that if the secret place in the depth of your heart is stuffed with all the hurt and the pain of wrong relationships, there will be no room for you to meet with your Groom, the Prince of Peace, in intimate fellowship.

Let me explain by giving you an example from my own life. When I was young, but old enough for love, I believed the lies of Lucifer and allowed someone to remove the corner of the King's garment. First, I listened to the lie that to be sexually active outside of marriage would fill the void in my heart. The world sold the lie to me, and my flesh bought into the deception. But no matter how close I was with someone, that person could not permanently fill the void in my life. I did not realize that only a *right relationship* with the Prince of Peace could fill the hole in my heart!

Eventually, when my life was out of control, I returned to the King and bowed my life before Him. In love, He began to teach me how to give the hurt and the pain to Him. He did this because He wanted nothing to come between the intimate relationship He desired to have with me. He was not willing to share the secret place in my heart with anyone or anything else, for He is a jealous King. In fact, El-Kanno, "the Jealous God," is one of His names (see Exodus 20:5).

Let me share with you an interesting adventure on which the King took me. I was living in Eastern Europe with my family in the country of Bulgaria when I was invited to teach at a woman's retreat in California. The theme for their weekend was *Hidden Treasures*. The moment I heard the theme, I was excited. What a fun theme! Hidden Treasures! I began to pray and ask the King what He desired me to teach these ladies. He began to impress on my heart that I should teach the difference between the true treasures we are to cherish in the secret place of our hearts and the old relics that we stuff and hoard there instead. *How interesting,* I thought. *Old relics.*

A short time later my family visited Nessebur, a beautiful town on the Black Sea coast that has a 3,000-year-old history. There is a rich Christian heritage in this old town, including about 40 partially surviving churches made of beautiful stone and adobe that can still be seen today. As I was reading about the influence of these churches, I discovered an interesting statement: "Mediaeval chronicles record that relics of saints were preserved in the church but were moved to Venice [Italy] in 1257."[2]

This caught my interest. My family and I had brought a Bulgarian friend with us that day, and I asked her what the old relics were. Were they gold? Jewels? Some other prized treasure? They must have been quite precious for someone to take the trouble to move them to Italy. My friend replied that they were not something we would consider important; in fact, they were old bones. Old bones! Why would anyone desire to keep *old bones*? Let alone move them around as if they were valuable treasures?

I could not forget my lesson in old relics that day. Soon after, my family and I moved back to America. Because of flight schedules, we ended up having a free day in Munich, Germany, so we visited Maximilian's residence. This is a historic castle that is amazing in its grandeur. We were in awe as we entered a room full of treasure chests. We passed by chests made of fine silver, gold, jewels and gems, each one being more splendid than the last. It was then that I realized the walls of the treasure chest were made of glass so you could see what the contents contained. To my horror, I discovered that inside the chests were old relics—old bones! One even contained the whole corpse of a baby. It was grotesque. Why would anyone want to keep old bones, let alone put them on display in glass treasure chests?

I don't mean any disrespect if this is practiced in your religion, but it was something that could not compute with my way of thinking! And yet, the King used this image to speak to me. He began to impress on my heart that *this is exactly what we do*. We stuff old relics deep within our hearts— deep within our inmost beings in the secret place—when we hoard the hurt and the pain of the past.

For you to fully understand what the King said to me, I need to give you a few definitions. First, "hoard" as a noun means "precious hidden accumulations [or collections],"[3] and as a verb it can also mean "to keep, as one's thoughts, to oneself."[4] So, "hoard" basically means to keep something in secret. This could include a precious hidden collection, or it could include hidden thoughts stuffed in a secret place. Of course, the word "stuff" as a verb means "to fill by packing things in; [or] to cram."[5] Furthermore, one noteworthy definition for "relic" is "survival from the past."[6]

When someone does something to hurt us deeply, we keep the pain to ourselves and think about the hurt over and over again. Then, when we can stand it no longer, we *stuff* and *hoard* these hurtful thoughts deep within our inmost being—deep within the secret place. There, we guard these relics like precious treasure. Consider this verse that one of the King's scribes wrote twice in the book of Proverbs:

> The words of a gossip are like choice morsels; they go down to a man's inmost parts.
> —Proverbs 18:8; 26:22

Why do the hurtful words of a gossip go down to our *inmost* parts? Because we do not know how to handle the hurt in the manner the King intended! So instead, we stuff and hoard it to escape from the pain of the past. This causes the hurts to become old relics within our hearts—"survival from the past." Without realizing it, over time these old relics become precious treasures to us.

Think about this for a moment. Why would anyone keep the corpse of a baby and display it in a beautiful treasure chest? Because the hurt and the pain they were experiencing made them unwilling to let it go. They did not know how to put the tragic event in its proper place, so they hoarded the bones until they became old relics. Eventually, these relics became precious to them.

We also stuff and hoard the hurt and pain of our past in beautiful treasure chests in the depths of our hearts. We keep them there in the secret place, as survival from the past, because we do not know what to do with them. But the King desires honesty within our hearts and truth in the depths of our inmost being. Listen to what the King's scribe David wrote: "Surely you desire truth in the inner parts; you teach me wisdom in the inmost place" (Psalm 51:6). We are to *treasure* and *cherish* the King's Word deep within so there is room for us to meet with the Prince of Peace in intimacy.

The word "treasure" means "to collect and store up for future use; [or even] to hoard."[7] When we store up the Word in our innermost place, it becomes a treasure that will lead us and guide us. This is why the psalmist wrote, "I have hidden your word in my heart that I might not sin against you" (Psalm 119:11). Unfortunately, all too often the old relics become the treasure we collect and store up for future use— often in ways we never imagined. This provides a tremendous stronghold for Lucifer, the betrayer, to use throughout our lives.

Let's examine these strongholds so you can better recognize them for what they are. I will begin by sharing honestly from my own life. Before I understood how to handle pain in the way the King intended (which I will share with you in my next letter), when someone did something to hurt me, I would stuff that hurt deep within my heart and keep it under lock and key. Over time, I began to treasure these old relics, without even realizing it. Thus, I was collecting and storing them up to be used in ways I never intended!

When the old relics of hurt and pain began to rot and decay, they manifested themselves into the sins of anger and bitterness. These are sins that I would not admit existed, even to myself, but I hoarded them just the same. I convinced myself that everything was fine, because I was too afraid to unlock the door to the secret place of my heart. Soon, the unconfessed sin of anger and bitterness began to poison and infect every aspect of my life, causing me to feel separated from the King.

As a result, when Lucifer then came and enticed me to eat the forbidden fruit of sex outside of marriage—to remove the garment of covering the King had placed over me for protection—I listened to the world and fell prey to his deception. The secret place within the depths of my heart was stuffed so full of the old relics that I could not hear the still, small voice of the King warning me to flee. This poison within my heart further fueled my sinful behavior, and at a young age I began looking for love in all the wrong places *as a means of surviving all the past hurt and pain* the old relics in my heart had created. But the Word declares:

> Surely the arm of the LORD is not too short to save, nor his ear too dull to hear. But your iniquities have separated you from your God; your sins have hidden his face from you, so that he will not hear.
>
> —Isaiah 59:1-2

My sin caused the void in my heart, which gave Lucifer the opening he was watching and waiting for. Of course, the King, in His wisdom, knew that stuffing and hoarding the hurt and pain of the past would be deadly to my soul. He knew the poison would spread throughout my body, especially to my heart—that special part of me that is *void* without a right relationship with Him. But praise the Lord! The King is good and full of love, grace and mercy. The moment I came to Him and asked forgiveness for trying to fill the void by searching for love in all the wrong places, He set me free. However, for years I was unaware that I still harbored the *other sins* of anger and bitterness deep in my heart. These were only in my thoughts, and I thought they were hidden from all to see.

I believed the old relics were safely hidden from view, but in reality they were much like the treasure chests made with clear glass. Those closest to me—those whom I loved dearly—could see the old decaying bones through my sinful attitudes and behaviors. It wasn't until I took the old relics of hurt and pain to the foot of the King's throne and left them there that I was set free from these strongholds.

Dear beloved, I do not know the circumstances in your life, but I do know how Lucifer works and how the world affects you. I know that you have been hurt. Yet, just as in my situation, if you do not handle these hurts correctly in the manner the King intended, they will begin to rot and decay, causing poison to infect your whole life—and your whole household. I must warn you: unless you learn how to give the old relics to the King in the manner He intended, Lucifer *will* use the old relics as a stronghold in your life. The old relics of hurt and pain are always a consequence of *sin*. Sometimes this is your own sin (such as in the case of bad decisions and foolish choices), but it can also be the result of another's sin against you (such as in the case of rape or abuse). Either way, when you choose to hang onto the old relics, the King considers it to be sin in His sight. Listen to His Word:

> Do not be deceived, God is not mocked; for whatever
> a man sows, that he will also reap.
> —Galatians 6:7, NKJV

When old relics of hurt and pain are not handled in the manner the King intended, they become *sin* in the depths of your innermost beings, because eventually they turn into anger and bitterness. That sin is like filthy rags in the sight of the King. Listen to what the King's scribe Isaiah wrote:

> All of us have become like one who is unclean, and all
> our righteous acts are like *filthy rags*.
> —Isaiah 64:6a, emphasis added

The term "filthy rags" in this verse refers to the cloth a woman used during her period—a time when she was considered "unclean."[8] We can act so righteous on the outside, but the King sees the filthy rags hidden within that make us unclean. Lucifer will lie to us and say that our filthy rags do not matter, but do not believe him—there are always consequences to our sins. Remember that it was Lucifer, as the serpent, who came to Adam and Eve and enticed them to eat of the forbidden fruit in the Garden of Eden. The King's Word tells us that the moment they did so, they reaped the consequences of their disobedience:

> Then the eyes of both of them were opened, and they
> realized they were *naked*; so they sewed fig leaves to-
> gether and made *coverings* for themselves. Then the
> man and his wife heard the sound of the LORD God
> as he was walking in the garden in the cool of the day,
> and they *hid* from the LORD God among the trees of
> the garden.
> —Genesis 3:7-8, emphasis added

Notice the italicized words in this passage: Adam and Eve immediately tried to *cover* their *nakedness* and *hide* from the King. But the King knew they needed to deal immediately with the filthy rags of the sin they had in their hearts. That's why He called to them in the Garden. That's why He asked them questions to get them thinking.

> The LORD God called to the man, "Where are you?" He answered, "I heard you in the garden, and I was afraid because I was naked; so I hid." And he said, "Who told you that you were naked? Have you eaten from the tree that I commanded you not to eat from?"
>
> —Genesis 3:9-11

Although thousands of years have passed since Adam and Eve lived in paradise, we still operate the same way today. We too try to cover, bury, stuff and hoard our sins, just as Adam and Eve did. You may be arguing right now and saying that you do not have any old relics (hurt and pain) or any filthy rags (anger and bitterness) hidden in the secret place in your heart—that all has been given to the King. According to the Word, we are very good at deceiving ourselves (see 1 John 1:8). But I must warn you that by hoarding the old relics of hurt and pain, they will eventually turn into the filthy rags of anger and bitterness. This is important, so let me repeat it in a slightly different way. When hurt is not handled in the manner the King intended, it will turn into the filthy rag of anger; which, in time, will turn into bitterness; which ultimately will turn into a bitter poison that will infect your whole life and cause you to be separated from your King; which will provide Lucifer, the schemer, with a tremendous stronghold.

It is of great importance to understand that this bitter poison—this infection—can fuel depression and anxiety when Lucifer shoots just the right fiery dart to remind you of the past. It can fuel outbursts of anger and over-protectiveness, which will rise up when you least expect it, leaving you feeling overwhelmed and out of control. It can create nightmares that repeat themselves again and again, no matter how safe you felt when you climbed into bed. It can lead to you using drugs and alcohol as a means of covering the pain so the hiding can continue. It can sabotage good relationships and make you to endure bad ones as a way of reinforcing feelings of unworthiness. It can lead to over-eating, over-spending, over-cleaning and over-anything—or just the opposite—as a way of punishing yourself.

If you struggle with any of these issues, you need to understand that they are tied to the old relics of hurt and pain in the depths of your heart. Stuffing and hoarding will not make the pain go away—this will just cause more hurt and pain, more rot and decay, which will increase the poison and infection in your life. Time doesn't heal a broken heart; it all depends on what you do with that time. Just think about the bones in the treasure chests in Maximilian's residence. Do you think the family keeping the old relics of a baby helped make the pain go away? Or did the hoarding of those old relics serve to increase and prolong the pain?

Learn a lesson from both Adam and Eve. It is impossible to hide from the truth, so don't try! The King desires you to know and understand what His scribe Ezekiel penned in His Word: He *bathed you with water*. He *washed the blood from you*. He *put ointments on you*. Note that the verbs *bathed*, *washed* and *put* are all in the past tense—it is already *done*. In view of this marvelous truth, the King desires you to walk in the freedom of the finished work. He doesn't want you to hold on to the old relics and filthy rags of the past. He desires truth in your innermost being. So fill the secret place of your heart with treasure worthy of who you are in Christ.

It is time for you to take responsibility for your actions—even the action of stuffing and hoarding. Look to the story of Adam and Eve in the Garden one more time:

> [The King] said, "Who told you that you were naked? Have you eaten from the tree that I commanded you not to eat from?" The man said, "The woman you put here with me—she gave me some fruit from the tree, and I ate it." Then the [King] said to the woman, "What is this you have done?" The woman said, "The serpent deceived me, and I ate."
>
> —Genesis 3:11-13

Did you see how both Adam and Eve tried to place the blame on anyone but themselves? They denied responsibility for their actions and tried to rationalize their decision to sin. Many times this is true in our lives. We refuse to take responsibility for our sin and rationalize it away or blame others for our actions. This just leads to us becoming angry and bitter. Listen to the Word one more time:

> All of us have become like one who is unclean, and all our righteous acts are like *filthy rags*.
>
> —Isaiah 64:6, emphasis added

> Son of man, when the people of Israel were living in their own land, they defiled it by *their conduct and their actions. Their conduct was like a woman's monthly uncleanness in my sight.*
>
> —Ezekiel 36:17, emphasis added

Our actions of blaming and rationalizing our sin are acts of unrighteousness. As we continue to hoard these old relics, they become like a woman's monthly uncleanness. When you truly think about it—it's disgusting! Worse yet, it gives Lucifer an even greater stronghold.

In the King's Word, the scribe Zechariah shows how the enemy was able to use old relics and filthy rags as a stronghold in the life of Joshua, who was a high priest of Israel. He writes:

> Then he showed me Joshua the high priest standing before the angel of the LORD, and Satan standing at his right side to accuse him. The LORD said to Satan, "The LORD rebuke you, Satan!" . . . . Now Joshua was dressed in *filthy clothes* as he stood before the angel.
> —Zechariah 3:1-3, emphasis added

Lucifer desired to have a stronghold in Joshua's life, but listen to what follows:

> The angel said to those who were standing before him, 'Take off his *filthy clothes.*" Then he said to Joshua, "See, I have taken away your sin, and I will put rich garments on you."
> —Zechariah 3:4, emphasis added

Remember that the King has said, "I bathed you with water and washed the blood from you and put ointments on you. I clothed you with an embroidered dress and put leather sandals on you. I dressed you in fine linen and covered you with costly garments" (Ezekiel 16:9-10). For you are clothed in righteousness.

Soon, I will find a way to get my next letters to you. Wait expectantly for them! They will be especially helpful to you if you struggle with any of the strongholds Lucifer sets up in a person's life—such as depression, anxiety, rage, overprotectiveness, nightmares, wrong relationships and/or other self-destructive behaviors. Remember, these come about as a result of stuffing and hoarding the old relics and filthy rags. But take heart, for the next two letters will contain the key to unlock the secret place filled with old relics and filthy rags.

The King wants to teach you how to leave them at the foot of His throne forever so you can be set free from the strongholds of Lucifer! Until that time, always remember that you are bathed with water—in fact, Living Water. Let it pour over you as you immerse yourself in it and say, *"I am bathed with water."*

Memorize the truth that you are washed clean. Lavish in the cleansing as you bubble aloud, *"I am washed clean."*

Know deep within your heart, in the secret place, that you are anointed with ointment. Begin healing as you declare, *"I am anointed with ointment."*

Best yet, as you heal you will be able to walk blameless. Walk forward as you claim, *"I am able to walk blameless."*

Always remember that you are the bride of Christ. You are engaged to the Prince of Peace! You are the Lord's, for He gave you His solemn oath. In view of this precious truth, claim it with confidence, *"I am His!"*

Washed clean for eternity,
Your Well-Adorned Servant

Chapter Thirteen

Adorned in the Leather Sandals of Peace

You Are at Peace with God

Prepare the way for the LORD. . . .
And the glory of the LORD will be revealed,
and all mankind together will see it.
Isaiah 40:3b,5a

*D*ear Beloved Believer,

Do you struggle with the consequences of sin that I described in my last letter? Did you uncover any old relics and filthy rags that you have hoarded in your heart—old relics such as hurt and pain, or filthy rags of anger and bitterness? It is the King's desire to shine the truth "on those living in darkness and in the shadow of death, to guide [your] feet into the path of peace" (Luke 1:79b). Can you honestly say that you are walking along that path of peace that surpasses understanding?

When you think of "peace," the words "calm," "quiet," "serene," "content" and "harmony" might come to mind. Are these words that describe your life? Or are your days filled with just the opposite—anxiety, worry, depression, conflict and tension? Peace is "the absence of anxiety."¹ Do you want your life to be absent of anxiety?

123

Well, it is my desire and my commission from the King to help guide your *feet into the path of peace*. Remember what the King's Word says:

> Be strong in the Lord and in the power of His might. Put on the whole armor of God, that you may be able to stand against the wiles of [Lucifer]. . . . Stand therefore . . . having shod your feet with the preparation of the gospel of peace.
>
> —Ephesians 6:10b-11,14-15, NKJV

I have found that Lucifer will use the old relics and filthy rags to create a stronghold in your life and cause you to be ineffective for the Kingdom. When this happens, depression, anxiety, outbursts of anger, relationship difficulties and many other self-destructive behaviors soon follow. Unfortunately, this makes it impossible for you to have peace and reflect the King's glory. As a result, you won't be able to stand firm *with the preparation of the gospel of peace*.

The word translated "preparation" in the Greek comes from the root word *hetoimaz*, which means to prepare or make ready.[2] Interestingly, it is this same root word that John the Baptist used when he cried out in the desert, "*Prepare* the way for the Lord" (Mark 1:3, Luke 3:4, emphasis added). It is your life, lived out in peace, that prepares the way for the gospel to be shared with those around you.

Now, as I have stated in my previous letters, there is a spiritual battle being waged all around you each day. Given this, it might seem odd that Paul, the King's inspired scribe, instructs you to *shod your feet with the preparation of the gospel of peace*. After all, a battlefield is a place filled with rage and hate, and you wouldn't expect to find peace in such a place. So, why did Paul use this imagery?

What Paul is revealing in this passage is how you are to *live* as you walk through this spiritual battlefield. The truth of the King's Word, when applied to your life, will bring peace. It is this peace that the King truly desires you to have deep within your heart—within the secret place—no matter how fierce the battle is raging around you.

Think about it: If you were on a hillside watching a fierce battle and you discovered that one person in the conflict was at total peace, would you not keep your eye on that individual? Would you not look to that person for guidance? Would you not desire what that person had? This is what you represent when you are at total peace in the midst of life's trials. This is what *prepares* the way for you to share the gospel with others and is how you reflect the King's glory to those around you. As you walk through the battlefield of life, others will be watching and trying to figure out how you can remain at total peace. In this way, you will prepare the way for them to find the King of Peace.

As with the other items in the armor of God, the leather sandals of peace were based on items a Roman soldier would wear. Now, for a Roman soldier to be able to stand firm during a fierce battle, he needed to have his feet fitted with the proper shoes. According to Danny Bond in *Clothed to Conquer*, one of the cleverer strategies used against the Romans "was to take wooden sticks and sharpen them down to razor-sharp points, which were jammed down into the ground [point up]. An entire field could be filled with these piercing stakes. . . . Once in place, they stuck just far enough above the ground to pierce the sole of the attacker's shoe, thereby rendering him unable to walk or stand."[3]

To protect the soldier from weapons that caused such disabling wounds, the Romans developed a shoe with an extra-thick and extra-strong sole made up of different layers of leather. When the soldier firmly fitted these sandals onto his feet with leather straps, he was protected from dangerous stakes hidden in the ground. In addition, the soles of the sandals had spikes—much like the cleats we find on sports shoes—that gave him a firm footing as he maneuvered about. So, the leather sandals gave the Roman soldier stability, mobility, balance and opportunity. If the solder was not fully equipped with these shoes, he could not stand firm.

The same is true today. If you are not fully clothed in the armor of the King—including the leather sandals of peace—you will be unable to stand against Lucifer's schemes. Your life will be unstable, due to anger, and out of balance, because of bitterness. This will impact your mobility and prevent you from moving forward in your walk as a believer. You will miss out on the opportunity to reflect the King's glory to those around you, and thus you will not prepare the way of the Lord.

Dear beloved, Lucifer would like nothing better than for you to be ineffective in the King's service. He will set stakes and traps to pierce your heart and soul, and it is his hope that you will leave these wounds unattended. In Paul's day, if a hidden stake injured a soldier and he did not tend to the wound, it would become infected and spread poison throughout the soldier's body. This is what Lucifer desires—for you to allow the hurt and pain you have experienced to create filthy rags of anger and bitterness that will decay and poison your life. Ultimately, this leads to spiritual death.

But there is hope. Remember what the King has said:

> I bathed you with water and washed the blood from
> you and put ointments on you. I clothed you with an
> embroidered dress and put leather sandals on you.
> —Ezekiel 16:9-10

The King wants to wash the old relics of hurt and pain with His healing ointment. He wants to soften and soothe

the filthy rags of anger and bitterness and transform them into soft and pliable sandals of peace. He wants to clothe you with an embroidered dress and put leather sandals on you so you can stand firm and reveal His glory. Remember that the equipment we are given is of divine origin and has the power to destroy *all* of Lucifer's strongholds:

> The weapons we fight with are not the weapons of the world. On the contrary, they have divine power to demolish strongholds. We demolish arguments and every pretension that sets itself up against the knowledge of God, and *we take captive every thought to make it obedient to Christ.*
>
> —2 Corinthians 10:4-5, emphasis added

By taking captive the old relics and filthy rags and making them obedient to the Prince of Peace, you will keep the infection and poison they create from setting in and spreading. This will prevent Lucifer from setting up a stronghold in your life and give you a strategic advantage in battle. When you equip the leather sandals of peace, you will have firm footing and mobility and be able to walk forward in peace.

As a believer in the King, it is critical that you learn the proper way of defending yourself in battle. When someone does or says something to hurt you, you must resist the natural inclination to stuff the hurt deep down within your heart in the secret place. If you do not immediately take the hurtful issues to the foot of the King's throne and leave them there, Lucifer will use this stronghold to cause you to stumble and fall.

Your enemy has no remorse or compassion, and when he discovers deep wounds in your heart, he will use them to increase the damage. He knows just when to twist that stake and shove it in a bit deeper! He will bombard you with additional blows, causing you to slowly die from a life filled with anger and bitterness. This is why you must resist stuffing your pain and anger. Note what Paul says in the King's Word:

> "In your anger do not sin": Do not let the sun go down while you are still angry, and do not give [Lucifer] a foothold.
>
> —Ephesians 4:26-27

If you allow the sun to go down on your anger, night after night that anger will slowly turn into bitterness. That bitterness, in turn, will decay into a bitter poison that will spread an infection throughout your heart. When that infection sets in, it will cause depression, anxiety, outbursts of anger, and many other consequences that will keep you from reflecting the King's glory to those who are watching you.

This is why the King's Word teaches that you must immediately deal with anger. Unresolved anger will make you unstable. It will cause you to lose your footing in the fight. It will impede your mobility and prevent you from moving forward in your walk as a believer. This is why the King's scribes write:

> Make every effort to live in peace with all men. . . . See to it that no one misses the grace of God and that no bitter root grows up to cause trouble and defile many.
>
> —Hebrews 12:14-15

> Make sure there is no man or woman, clan or tribe among you today whose heart turns away from the LORD our God . . . make sure there is no root among you that produces such bitter poison.
>
> —Deuteronomy 29:18

Unless you take the hurtful thoughts captive—moment by moment on a daily basis—and make them obedient to the Prince of Peace, your life will be out of balance. One definition of "balance" is "a state of harmony,"[4] so when your life is out of balance, it means you are out of harmony with the King! This will prevent you from preparing the way for the gospel of peace, and you will lose the opportunity to reflect the King's glory. Remember that this is one of the reasons why you were given life.

Think about it: when you see someone who is always down and blue, and yet that person claims to be a child of the King, is he or she really reflecting the King's glory? Or what about a person who screams and yells in rage, yet he or she also claims to be a believer? Is that individual preparing the way of the Lord in his or her actions and deeds? Be warned and be aware—others are watching.

So today, dear beloved, examine your heart to see if there is any unresolved anger or bitterness that you have stored there. Don't just assume that all is well deep within the secret place, for the King's Word says that "the heart knows its own bitterness" (Proverbs 14:10a, NKJV). Be honest with yourself and be "aware of the afflictions of [your] own heart" (1 Kings 8:38). Remember that the deeper the wound, the greater the poison.

Once you identify any old relics of hurt and pain and any filthy rags of anger and bitterness, leave them at the foot of the King's throne. To do this, simply bow your heart in prayer. Prayer is the King's top-secret communication system, and it grants you instant access to your Commander. This is war, and if you are not able to communicate with your King, you will not be victorious. You also cannot be victorious if you are bogged down under the weight of these filthy rags. Remember what they represent—*the cloths a woman uses during her period*. Yuck! So leave them at the foot of the King's throne.

Over the years as I have taught this principle, I have heard many people say that they cannot feel or touch the hurt, pain, anger and bitterness. Many of them realize these old relics and filthy rags are there, but they cannot physically feel or touch them, so they do not know how to give them over the King. In fact, it is true that these old relics and filthy rags are often *intangible*. However, there is something tangible that you *can* do to help you deal with these issues: write a letter to the person with whom you are angry.

Now, I want to stress that this will *not be something that you will actually mail to that person*—the letter is between you and the King *only*. It is extremely important for you to follow this rule, for if you were to give the letter to the person, it would just create another stronghold for Lucifer to exploit. Instead, I want you to use the letter as a tool to set you free and give you peace in the midst of battle. I want you to use it as a key to unlock the secret place in your heart and release the old relics and filthy rags that are hidden there. So take a moment to get a piece of paper and a pen, find a quiet place, and kneel at the foot of the throne. Write Psalm 139:23-24 at the top of the page, and as you do make it your prayer to the King:

> Search me, O God, and know my heart; test me and know my anxious thoughts. See if there is any offensive way in me, and lead me in the way everlasting.

It's interesting to note that the word "offensive" can also be translated as "hurtful," "wicked" or "grievous." In view of this, ask the King if there is any hurtful, offensive, wicked or grievous way in you. After that, address the letter to whomever the King is impressing on your heart, and then write out everything you would say to the person if you lived in a perfect world. Do not hold anything back, for you cannot hide anything from the King—He is omniscient and already knows the old relics and filthy rags that have been festering in your heart. If you begin to cry, just let the tears flow, because it means the King is washing your heart. Don't try to stop them, as this might prevent you from hearing what the Royal Counselor is softly trying to say to you. The tears are cleansing the secret place deep within so that there will be room to meet with your Prince of Peace!

Your letter may be long or short. One time when I was teaching about this tool at a retreat, a woman came up to me and said, "I just wrote 26 pages, and I've been set free!" Many others have shared that they needed to write more than one letter to different people. Regardless, the important thing is to go to the King in prayer, ask Him to reveal the hurt, pain, anger and bitterness, and move forward in victory. Take the mountain captive! Allow the Royal Counselor to give you strength as you write.

When you have finished writing your letter, offer the old relics and the filthy rags as a fragrant sacrifice to the King of kings. Remember that the King offered His Son, the Prince of Peace, as a sacrifice so that you could have eternal life. Therefore, as Paul says, "Live a life of love, just as Christ loved us and gave himself up for us as a fragrant offering and sacrifice to God" (Ephesians 5:2). I want you to literally find a fireplace (or, better yet, a fire pit), set the letter on fire, and watch the smoke rise to the King. This act, dear beloved, is *tangible*. This is something you can touch and see as you give it to the King!

When the old relics and the filthy rags are destroyed, Lucifer and his armed forces will never again be able to use them against you to poison and infect your life. The stronghold will be broken, freeing you from all the terrible issues we have talked about (such as depression and anxiety), and you will be able to move forward in peace! But be warned:

once again, the King loves you so deeply that He gives you a choice. You can choose to leave the old relics and filthy rags at the foot of His throne, or you can choose to hold on to them. Which will it be?

As you begin this process, my prayer is that you will spend some quiet time at the foot of the King's throne and be brave enough to write the letter. I join the apostle Paul in saying, "I pray that out of [the King's] glorious riches he may strengthen you with power through his Spirit in your inner being" (Ephesians 3:16). I pray that you will equip yourself with the leather sandals of peace so that you will have stability, mobility and balance, and so that you will be able to prepare the way of the Lord to shine forth the gospel of peace. I pray that Paul's words in Romans 10:15 will become true in your life: "How beautiful are the feet of those who bring good news!"

Until my next letter, remember that you are able to walk in peace no matter where the King leads you. Boldly claim it: *"I am able to walk in peace."*

As you offer up the old relics and filthy rags as a burnt offering, you will be at peace with the King. Embrace the comfort in the secret place, deep within your inmost being, as you whisper, *"I am at peace with the King."*

As you release the old relics and filthy rags, you will be equipping your feet with the preparation of the gospel of peace so you can stand firm. Stand boldly as you come to understand it: *"I am able to stand firm."*

Never forget that the King Himself preserves your life and keeps your feet from slipping so that you can prepare the way for the gospel of peace. The King reigns! So shout with confidence: *"I am victorious!"*

Basking in His wonderful peace,
Your Steadfast Servant

Chapter Fourteen

Wearing Costly Garments

You Are Set Free

*I dressed you in fine linen
and covered you with costly garments.*
Ezekiel 16:10b

*D*ear Beloved Believer,

In my last letter, I told you how to be free of two of the filthy rags that you may have stuffed deep within your heart: anger and bitterness. But be warned! There is one more filthy rag that you must be rid of in your life. This last filthy rag is one that will shackle you and hold you captive if you do not choose to completely do away with it. Worse yet, by keeping it, you will eventually *take back* the previous filthy rags of anger and bitterness and, more than likely, the old relics of hurt and pain will come back with a vengeance as well. What is this rag? It is the rag of *unforgiveness.*

As with anger and bitterness, the King has made a way for you to be free of this last filthy rag. But again, with the King's freedom comes a choice. You can choose to imitate the King and live a life of love, or you can choose to remain where you are, shackled in a prison and chained to unforgiveness. Listen to what the King's scribe Paul wrote about this in the Word:

> Be imitators of God, therefore, as dearly loved chil-
> dren and live a life of love, just as Christ loved us and
> gave himself up for us as a fragrant offering and sac-
> rifice to God.
>
> —Ephesians 5:1-2

It is my prayer that you will know deep within your heart—deep within the secret place—that the King loves you and that you will accept His offer of freedom. It is my prayer that you will move this knowledge from your head to your heart so you will apply it to your life and begin to walk in wisdom. It is also my prayer that you will make the choice to be an imitator of the King and live a life of love. One of the ways to do this is to follow your King in the way He has shown forgiveness to you. Look at another passage that the scribe Paul wrote in the King's Word:

> Be kind and compassionate to one another, *forgiving
> each other*, just as in Christ God forgave you.
>
> —Ephesians 4:32, emphasis added

When you accepted the Prince of Peace as your Lord and Savior, the King bestowed His unconditional forgive-ness upon you. He forgave all your sins—past, present and future. Now, as His imitator, He calls *you* to forgive all the wrongs that have been done to you—past, present and future. Remember that filthy rags represent "the cloths a woman uses during her period,"[1] and the King no longer wants any of these to remain in your heart. Furthermore, He knows that by clinging to this filthy rag, you will be unable to love others in the way that He loves you and that you will not have the peace He wants you to have.

So, the question you must ask yourself is, *Am I hoard-ing or treasuring any unforgiveness deep within the secret place in my heart?* Be completely honest with yourself as you an-swer this question. Remember the King is omniscient—He knows everything, and you cannot fool Him! It is time to stop making excuses for why you can't forgive, for excuses will only keep you from freedom; and it is time to stop blaming others, for blame is just another word for sin. It is time to embrace the moment-by-moment daily decision to die to your self and *choose* to forgive others.

Now, you may be arguing that what I am telling you to do is impossible. After all, I have not been in your situation, and I do not know the wrongs that were done against you. This is true! On your own, it would be impossible for you to forgive others. But, as I have said, *you are not on your own*. You have the Royal Counselor by your side, and as Paul writes, "I can do all things through him who strengthens me" (Philippians 4:13, ESV). Rely on Him to give you everything you need to be an imitator of the King.

The unfortunate truth is that forgiveness has a cost—a very high cost. When you make the decision to forgive another person, you will pay a price—the price of dying to self, dying to your rights, and dying to your desires. However, unlike the Prince of Peace, your choice to forgive will not cost *your physical life*. As Warren Wiersbe writes, "It was love that motivated the Father to give His Son [the Prince of Peace] to be the Savior of the world (John 3:16; Rom. 5:8; 1 John 4:9-10), and it was love that motivated the Son to give his life for the sins of the world (John 15:13)."[2] The Prince of Peace paid the price of His own life to offer Himself as fragrant offering for your sins. Without this sacrifice, your sins could not have been forgiven. This was the *most costly decision ever made*— and it was made completely out of love for you.

It is interesting to note that just as the King gives you the choice to be a part of His plan in forgiving others, He gave the Prince of Peace a choice as to whether He wanted to be a part of the King's plan to forgive you. To fully understand this, let's take a peek at the final few hours of the Prince's life. The night before He was betrayed, He was praying in the Garden of Gethsemane. He already knew what was about to take place, and He was greatly distressed about what He was being asked to endure. As the physician Luke describes the scene:

> Being in anguish, [the Prince of Peace] prayed more earnestly, and his sweat was like drops of blood falling to the ground.
>
> —Luke 22:44

The weight of the choice the Prince of Peace was facing caused Him so much anguish that He sweat drops of blood. It is important for you to understand that He had a choice. He did not have to go through with the King's plan. He did not need to atone for His *own* sin, because the King's Word says He was sinless. But out of love, your Prince made the decision to atone for *your* sin. He told His Father, the King, "Yet not my will, but yours be done" (Luke 22:42b).

To further prove to you that the King's Son had a choice in this matter, let us pick up the story where Judas is about to betray Him:

> So Judas came to the grove, guiding a detachment of soldiers and some officials from the chief priests and Pharisees. They were carrying torches, lanterns and weapons. *[The Prince of Peace], knowing all that was going to happen to him*, went out and asked them, "Who is it you want?" "Jesus of Nazareth," they replied. "I am he," Jesus said. . . . When Jesus said, "I am he," they drew back and fell to the ground.
>
> —John 18:3-6, emphasis added

As Pastor Jon Corson explains, when the King's Son says, "I am he," He is actually saying, "'I AM,' *'Ego Eimi'*—a

136

declaration of deity."[3] Your Prince was claiming—and rightfully so—that He was God. But notice what then happens: "With torches flying, armor clanking, and swords falling, [the soldiers] go down under the sheer power of Jesus' proclamation."[4] They draw back and fall to the ground! The soldiers had come "to arrest a meek peasant and instead were met in the dim light by a majestic person."[5] Jesus, your Prince of Peace, was in complete control at all times. He had a choice, and He paid the price of that choice with His life. That is the price of the Prince's forgiveness for you!

This cost was so great that at one point while the Prince of Peace was hanging on the cross, the King had to totally separate Himself from the Son. Remember in a prior letter that I said the King, God the Father, cannot look upon sin. When the Prince of Peace took your sin and my sin upon Himself, the King had to turn His back on the one He loved. It was at that moment the Prince cried out, "My God, my God, why have you forsaken me?" (Matthew 27:46b). Can you hear His cry? Why did He do it? Because of the depth of love He has for you. It was the price He was willing to pay to clothe you in costly garments and fine linen so you could be righteous.

The Prince's love for you was so deep that it literally broke His heart. Let me explain. The Prince of Peace was crucified on the day before Passover. This was a holy day for the Jewish people, and they did not want the bodies of the crucified left up on the crosses. So they asked Pilate, the ruling Roman authority in the region, to break the men's legs to speed up their deaths. Why? Because they knew that if the crucified men's legs were broken, they could no longer lift themselves up to breathe, and death by asphyxiation would occur. Here is how the King's scribe John describes what followed:

> The soldiers therefore came and broke the legs of the first man who had been crucified with Jesus, and then those of the other. But when they came to Jesus and found that he was already dead, they did not break his legs. Instead, one of the soldiers pierced Jesus' side with a spear, bringing a sudden flow of blood and water. . . . These things happened so that the scriptures would be fulfilled: "Not one of his bones will be broken," and, as another scripture says, "They will look on the one they have pierced."
>
> —John 19:32-34,36-37

Why was it so important that not one of the Prince's bones was broken? As Pastor Courson explains, "[Blood is] produced in the bone. Therefore, God mandated not a bone of His would be broken, ensuring a perpetual and inexhaustible supply of blood. That's why Paul could later declare, 'Where sin abounds, grace abounds yet more' (Romans 5:20). Truly, the blood of [your Prince of Peace] is sufficient to cleanse you from every sin you have ever committed or will commit. Why? Because not a bone of His was broken."[6] According to the King's Word, "Without the shedding of blood there is no forgiveness of sins" (Hebrews 9:22b, ESV). The blood of your Prince still covers and atones for you today so you could be forgiven for all your sins—past, present and future.

Even more striking in John's account is that Jesus was *already dead* by the time the Roman soldiers came to break the men's legs. As *Halley's Bible Handbook* notes, "[The Prince of Peace] was already dead when the spear pierced his side, after being on the cross six hours. Some medical authorities have said that in the case of heart rupture, and in that case only, the blood collects in the pericardium, the lining around the wall of the heart, and divides into a sort of bloody clot and a watery serum. If this is a fact, then the actual immediate physical cause of Jesus' death was heart rupture. . . . It may be that Jesus literally died of a heart broken over the sin of the world."[7] Do you understand what this means? *The Prince of Peace literally died of a broken heart!*

Perhaps, dear beloved, the Prince's heart did not break because the sin of the world was placed upon Him or because He was separated from the Father. Perhaps, instead, His heart broke because He knew there would be many who would not accept His gift of love. Have you ever loved someone so deeply but not had that love returned? Did your heart not feel as if it would break? Perhaps this is what happened to the Prince of Peace—His heart broke because you and I denied His love.

The price of your forgiveness and freedom was costly in so many ways. It was filled with sacrifice and love. In view of this, is the price of forgiving others that the King is asking you to pay so costly? If the Prince could pay the price to forgive you from all unrighteousness, could you not be an imitator of the King and choose to forgive those who have hurt you as well?

It is not always easy to make the choice to forgive another person, and it is one often entered into with tears. But it is only when you are willing to accept the gift—the sacrifice that was made for you—that you are able to understand the King's generous plan of forgiveness. Listen to what Wiersbe has to say: "During [Christ's] ministry, he both preached and practiced forgiveness. He said, 'But if you do not forgive men their sins, your Father will not forgive your sins' (Matthew 6:15). This doesn't mean that forgiveness is based on our good works, or that we earn God's forgiveness by forgiving others. . . . His prayer reminds us that if we're unwilling to forgive others, then our hearts are in no condition to ask

God for his forgiveness. If I'm broken before God, then I'll be forgiving towards others."[8]

Let me share another story from the King's Word—a parable the Prince of Peace told as a result of a question that Peter had concerning the forgiveness of others. We can learn much from this story.

> Therefore, the kingdom of heaven is like a king who wanted to settle accounts with his servants. As he began the settlement, a man who owed him ten thousand talents was brought to him. Since he was not able to pay, the master ordered that he and his wife and his children and all that he had be sold to repay the debt.
>
> The servant fell on his knees before him. "Be patient with me," he begged, "and I will pay back everything." The servant's master took pity on him, *canceled the debt* and let him go.
>
> But when that servant went out, he found one of his fellow servants who owed him a hundred denarii. He grabbed him and began to choke him. "Pay back what you owe me!" he demanded.
>
> "His fellow servant fell to his knees and begged him, "Be patient with me, and I will pay you back."
>
> *But he refused.* Instead, he went off and had the man thrown into prison until he could pay the debt.
>
> —Matthew 18:23-30, emphasis added

How ungrateful was that man who received grace and forgiveness for his debt. Yet, refused to be just as gracious! If we are truly honest with ourselves, isn't that what we do when we choose not to forgive a person who hurt us? We accept what the King has to offer—His wonderful forgiveness of *our* sins—but then we choose to turn around and cling to the filthy rag of unforgiveness as we nurture our grudge and hold onto our so-called rights. Who do we think we are?

Are we any better than the King? Even in this we need to cry out, "Lord, forgive us for our iniquities!" And then repent by changing our ways.

Dear beloved, forgiveness is not an option. It is a step of obedience—a step of obedience to the King of kings. By taking this step, you toss aside the filthy rag of unforgiveness that has cluttered your heart and begin to walk in *practical righteousness*. As I have mentioned in a prior letter, this is what you are to be busy doing as you wait for the Prince's return. This is the fine linen that represents the righteous deeds of the saints that you are to put on each and every day. What a picture—a practical picture—of removing the filthy rags and adorning the fine linen of righteousness!

The King has commanded you to take every thought captive—even thoughts of unforgiveness—and make them obedient to the Prince of Peace. The word "obedient" in the original Greek means "compliance or submission."[9] The word "submission" means agreeing to abide by the authority or control of another.[10] So, when you submit to your King's authority and place the filthy rag of unforgiveness at the foot of His throne, you comply—which simply means to act as ordered[11]—with His command to forgive. In this way, you rid your heart of filthy rags and unrighteousness and make a place where you can meet with your King.

The King asks you to take this step of obedience because He knows that forgiveness will be incredibly beneficial *to you*. Forgiveness may or may not change the other person who has wronged you, but it will definitely change you. Why? Because unforgiveness, like anger and bitterness, is a bitter poison that will infect your own life. For this reason, when you forgive others, you do so for *your own sake*. This is why the King says, "I, even I, am he who blots out your transgressions, *for my own sake*, and remembers your sins no more" (Isaiah 43:25, emphasis added). If the King forgives your sins for *His own sake*, then you must also live a life of love and follow after the King's example, as an imitator, and forgive for *your own sake*.

At this moment, perhaps you are convinced that you need to get rid of unforgiveness, but you now realize you have no idea how to do so in a practical manner. Maybe you have held on to the bitter poison of unforgiveness for so long that even though you are tired of it, it has become comfortable to you. It is as if this filthy rag has transformed into a filthy, stinky, disgusting old security blanket! Once again, the key to letting go of unforgiveness can be found in the King's Word. Listen to what your own Prince of Peace has said about how to let go of this old rotting rag:

> But I say to you who hear, love your enemies, do good to those who hate you, bless those who curse you, *pray for those who mistreat you*. . . . Be merciful, just as your Father is merciful.
> —Luke 6:27-28,36, NASB, emphasis added

When the Prince of Peace was being crucified, He prayed, "Father, forgive them, for they do not know what they do" (Luke 23:34b, NKJV). As Wiersbe notes, "Consider the wonder of the appeal. The tense of the verb 'said' indicates that our Lord repeated this prayer. As the soldiers nailed him to the cross, he prayed, 'Father, forgive them.' When they lifted the cross and placed it in the hole in the ground, our Lord prayed, 'Father, forgive them.' As he hung there between heaven and earth, and heard religious people mocking him, he repeatedly prayed, 'Father, forgive them.'"[12] As an imitator of the King, you need to follow the Prince's example and *pray* that the Father will forgive those who have mistreated you. *Praying* for those who have wronged you is the key to your freedom!

Like the other filthy rags, if there is unforgiveness in your heart, Lucifer will use it to create a stronghold. He will shoot his fiery darts at the infected area in an attempt to spread the poison deeper into your life. This is why prayer is so critical, because it *extinguishes* the fiery darts. So, whenever the enemy reminds you of the past, instead of dwelling on all the thoughts and feelings associated with your hurt, just pray for the person. *Pray for those who have mistreated you.* If the person is not saved, pray for his or her salvation. If the person is saved, pray for him or her to draw closer to the King. Pray for the person, give your hurt to the King, and move forward in victory.

Now, more than likely you won't *feel* like praying for the other person. In fact, you're more likely to feel like Jonah did when the King commanded him to warn the people of Nineveh of their destruction. Jonah didn't want the Ninevites to be rescued, and you may feel the same about the person who has wronged you. But remember that forgiveness is a step of *obedience*, not a feeling. It is the key to unlocking the prison cell that unforgiveness creates so you can walk in freedom and be clothed in the costly garments of righteousness.

In my own life, I have found that whenever I was reminded of the wrong that was done to me, as I have been obedient to pray for those who mistreated me, the forgiveness has come. When this occurs, the act of prayer is no longer *just* an act of obedience, and the forgiveness in my heart is complete. What wonderful freedom! Prayer has thus become my weapon of choice whenever someone does something to hurt me.

Remember that "the weapons we fight with"—including prayer—"have divine power to demolish strongholds" (2 Corinthians 10:4). So today, I want to encourage you to use prayer as a mighty weapon to demolish the stronghold of unforgiveness. Take strength from the knowledge that you can forgive because the King forgave you. In view of this liberation, take a step of obedience and vow, *"I am able to forgive."*

You have the power to be an imitator of the King through the power of the Holy Spirit, your Royal Counselor. Let Him hear you mimic it: *"I am an imitator of the King."*

You have the strength to walk in obedience. For this reason, stand firm as you walk forward and claim it: *"I am able to walk in obedience."*

Know that you can do all things through Him who strengthens you. State it with confidence: *"I am able to do all things through Him who strengthens me."*

Until the time I can write again, enjoy your newfound freedom, which leads to victory.

Worth the sacrifice,
Your Liberated Servant

Chapter Fifteen

Equipped with the Shield of Faith

You Are Protected by the King

Under his wings you will find refuge;
his faithfulness is a shield and buckler.
You will not fear the terror of night,
nor the arrow that flies by day.
Psalm 91:4b-5, ESV

$\mathcal{D}$ear Beloved Believer,

Have you ever struggled with your thought life? Have you ever had thoughts that you knew were not pleasing to the King? Perhaps the more you tried to stop them, the worse the wrong thinking became. It was as if something was fueling the flames! Well, as I have stated in my previous letters, Lucifer will shoot his arrows at you, and you need a way to defend yourself from his attack. This is what equipping yourself with the shield of faith is all about. Let's look once again at Paul's message in Ephesians:

> Finally, my brethren, be strong in the Lord and in the power of His might. Put on the whole armor of God, that you may be able to stand against the wiles of [Lucifer]. . . . Stand therefore, having girded your waist with truth, having put on the breastplate

of righteousness, and having shod your feet with the
preparation of the gospel of peace; above all, taking the
shield of faith with which you will be able to quench
all the fiery darts of [Lucifer] the wicked one.
　　　　　　　　　—Ephesians 6:10-11,14-16, NKJV

Notice that Paul cautions you *above all* to pick up the
shield of faith. The phrase "above all" reveals that the shield
of faith is extremely significant and is of utmost importance,
for it is your faith, lived out each day, that will help you
stand firm in the face of adversity and become all the King
created you to be. Your shield of faith will enable you to hold
fast to the King when Lucifer comes at you with his schemes
and tries to destroy your intimate relationship.

There are actually two types of faith: *saving faith* and
living faith. We have already discussed saving faith—it is
the faith you utilized when you made the decision to accept
the Prince of Peace as your Savior. *Living faith* is the faith
you use each day in your walk with the King. This faith is
an active, daily trust in the nature, character and love of
the King made known to you through His Word. It is from
this type of faith that you receive the strength and power to
stand firm in your King, who is your shield. Listen to what
the scribe David said in the Word:

> O Lord, how many are my foes! Many are rising
> against me; many are saying of my soul, there is no sal-
> vation for him in God. But you, O Lord, are a shield
> about me, my glory, and the lifter of my head.
> 　　　　　　　　　—Psalm 3:1-3, ESV

The shield of faith, when used properly, will protect your life.
It will quench "all the fiery darts of [Lucifer] the wicked one."
Furthermore, all of the other pieces of the King's armor will not
function properly without it. For this reason, it is important to understand how to equip yourself with the shield of faith each day.

Back in Paul's time, the Roman soldiers were often faced with enemies who used fiery arrows and fiery darts against them. The arrows had metal tips, and the enemy would wrap these tips in swabs of cotton and soak them in flammable pitch. The enemy would then light these fiery arrows and shoot them at an opposing solider. When an arrow hit its target, it would embed into the victim's body. The pitch would splatter, causing the soldier's body to burst into flames. In this way, if the soldier did not die from the impact of the arrow, he would die an agonizing death by burning. Another tactic was to dip the tip of an arrow into poison. If the arrow even nicked a man, the poison would go under his skin, and he would eventually die. Either of these two lethal arrows had the potential to kill a soldier if it struck its mark.

To defend against these lethal arrows, the Romans constructed a shield about the size of a small door—two feet by four feet—made of wood covered with leather or metal. The edges of this shield were constructed in such a way that it could interlock with other shields and create a solid wall. This wall of shields served as a place where the Roman soldier could be protected from the onslaught of fiery arrows, for the weapons of the enemy could not penetrate this defense. It is this type of shield that the King's scribe Paul was speaking about when he wrote the book of Ephesians.

Your shield of faith, like the Roman soldier's shield, serves as an impenetrable wall where you can hide to protect yourself from the fiery darts of the enemy. Just as the psalmist cried out to the King, "Hide me in the shadow of your wings" (Psalm 17:8, ESV), you can hide in the safety of the King, who is a shield around you. You can take refuge in Him, for "his faithfulness is a shield and buckler," and in Him "you will not fear the terror of night, nor the arrow that flies by day" (Psalm 91:4b-5, ESV). Through your *faith in the King*, the fiery darts will be quenched!

Now, remember that Lucifer is extremely intelligent and cunning in his attacks. He will bombard you with fiery darts aimed specifically at your faith so he can gradually wear you down. He will use both poison and fire in his arsenal, first dipping the tips of his arrows into poisonous lies and then igniting them and launching them at your heart and mind. When the arrows hit their mark, they explode and stir up lusts of the heart, or influence your emotions, or cut you down with discouragement and hopelessness. Let's take a look at each of these three types of attack.

The enemy's darts that stir up *lusts of the heart* trigger selfish desires. This can be a desire for money or material objects, or the desire for love and romance, or even lusts of the flesh. Many times, these false longings and desires begin when a fiery dart hits your heart and mind and begins to sever your intimate relationship with the King. These false longings and desires catch hold, and before you know it, your thought life is totally out of control. It's like a raging fire within your mind, destroying everything within its path—including your heart relationship with the King. You no longer desire to spend time with Him, but instead dwell upon your thought life, which is raging out of control.

If you do not get your thought life in order, your mind will be like a raging wildfire burning out of control. From afar, the wildfire can actually look beautiful, with colors of orange and gold glowing bright. But close up, it's terrible and destructive. It annihilates everything in its path and destroys property and lives. This is what happens when you allow thoughts of lust and greed to take hold and burn out of control—at first they seem innocent and intriguing, but then they annihilate and destroy your intimate relationship with the King. To combat this attack, you must set your heart on things above and not on earthly desires. As Paul instructs:

> Set your hearts on things above, where Christ is seated at the right hand of God. Set your minds on things above, not on earthly things. For you died, and your life is now hidden with Christ in God.
>
> —Colossians 3:1-3

Remember that you are hidden in the King's Son, the Prince of Peace, and He will protect you from this attack. So if you struggle in this area, pick up your shield of faith and set your heart on things above. Focus on the truth of the King's Word:

> Finally, brothers, whatever is true, whatever is honorable, whatever is just, whatever is pure, whatever is lovely, whatever is commendable, if there is any excellence, if there is anything worthy of praise, *think about these things.*
>
> —Philippians 4:8, ESV, emphasis added

The enemy's darts that *influence your emotions* can render you ineffective on the battlefield if you are unprepared. For this type of attack, Lucifer will dip his arrows into poisonous lies and target any area he believes is vulnerable. If you do not have your shield of faith ready, equipped and at hand, these arrows can hit the target of your mind when you least expect it and cause damage to your very being.

Note that Lucifer will often launch this type of attack when your defenses are down. He and his cohorts are always watching for an opportunity to shoot their fiery arrows, and when they find a vulnerable spot, the darts will come fast and swift. These onslaughts can seem never-ending, and you may be tempted to just give up the fight. As Danny Bond writes, "This is when we find that our shield is real. It's to be used against a real person, Satan or one of his cohorts, not just some unknown force. We are dealing with beings that move, think, strategize, and observe. Studying each of us, they look for weak points; and when they discover one, they attack."[1]

One of the weapons that Lucifer will use to target your emotions is the dart of fear and worry. When this arrow hits its mark, it causes you to look at your circumstances and begin to doubt that the King is protecting you and caring for you. When fear or worry takes hold in your heart, it pushes out faith, for the two cannot coexist. Faith *ends* where worry *begins*.

The dart of doubt will cause you to question the tenets of your faith—even to the point that you begin to doubt your salvation. Lucifer and his cohorts will often follow this up with the dart of guilt, reminding you of all the wrong that you have done in the past and causing you to doubt the King's forgiveness. If you continue to dwell on your past, you can fall into a deep pit of depression.

Another of Lucifer's frequently-used arrows is the dart of confusion. When confusion abounds, know that Lucifer is the cause. The King is *not* the author of confusion—in fact, His Son, the Prince of Peace, is known as the Author of Life, the Author of Salvation and, best yet, the Author of our Faith!

A final arrow that Lucifer will target at your emotions is the dart of self-pity. This attack is extremely destructive, for when it catches hold, it will ignite whatever it touches. Do not allow this to happen! Instead, set your mind on things above and not on fear, worry, doubt, guilt, depression, confusion or self-pity. Whenever you feel these emotions rising within you, give them immediately to the King, put on your breastplate of righteousness, and pick up your shield of faith. Remember, the Prince of Peace has covered all your sins with His blood and has clothed you in righteousness. You have been hidden in the King's Son, the Prince of Peace, who is your shield.

A third category of darts the enemy uses against you is *discouragement and hopelessness*. These darts are often aimed directly at your finances, your health, your relationships, and your very will to follow the King. We see this type of attack clearly in the story of Job. When the King asked Lucifer, "Where have you come from?" he answered, "From roaming through the earth and going back and forth in it" (Job 1:7b, 2:2b). Lucifer was looking for someone to devour! After *receiving permission to afflict Job*, Lucifer took away all of the possessions that Job held dear, including his children and his servants. Later, Lucifer attacked Job's health, and he was afflicted "with painful sores from the soles of his feet to the top of his head" (Job 2:7b). Lucifer attacked Job's *finances*, his *health* and his *relationships*.

At one point, Job's friends tried to convince him that he had done something wrong to warrant all of these misfortunes. Even Job's wife said to him, "Are you still holding on to your integrity? Curse God and die!" (Job 2:9b). This was Lucifer's ultimate goal: to bombard Job with fiery darts of discouragement to the point that Job *gave up his will* to follow the King. But Job did not lower his shield of faith for one moment. Although everything he had was gone, he still chose to put his faith in the King and follow Him in spite of his circumstances. He said:

> Naked I came from my mother's womb, and naked I will depart. The LORD gave and the LORD has taken away; may the name of the LORD be praised.
> —Job 1:21b

Imagine how it must have pleased the King to see that no matter what Lucifer threw at Job, he kept his faith. Job did not give up his will to please the King, even though he was facing crisis after crisis. This is one of the reasons you were given life—to please the King—and faith is the key to making this happen. In fact, the Word says, "Without faith it is impossible to please God" (Hebrews 11:6).

So take heart and be encouraged that Lucifer had to have the *King's permission* to shoot these fiery darts at Job. The King loves you deeply, and He will never allow anything to happen to you that He has not first sifted through His love. If the King allows a terrible trial to occur in your life, He does so for a reason; and He will not only give you the strength and the power to endure it but, better yet, you will also grow and mature in the midst of it (see James 1:2-4). In view of this fact, pick up your shield of faith and walk forward in battle. For you are able to walk by faith, and *not* by sight (see 2 Corinthians 5:7).

There is one more point I want to share with you about the Roman soldier's shield to encourage you in battle. Many times, a Roman soldier would dip his shield in water before the fight so that it would *immediately* quench the flaming arrows. Learn from this! You can also dip your shield of faith into the water—the Living Water—to quench the enemy's attacks. By immersing yourself in the Word each day and having an intimate and trusting relationship with the Prince of Peace, you will be prepared whenever Lucifer tries to aim his fiery arrows at your heart.

In closing, remember the words that the King said to a man named Abraham: "Do not be afraid, [Abraham]. I am your shield, your very great reward" (Genesis 15:1b). The King made a *promise* to *protect* and *provide* for Abraham, and Abraham trusted in this promise. For this reason, Paul said that "Abraham's faith was credited to him as righteousness" (Romans 4:9b). *Living faith* is trusting in the promises and the power of the King, and when you rely on Him in spite of your circumstances, it will be credited to you as righteousness. As you walk in faith, you will live out *practical righteousness* each day and strengthen your relationship with the King.

With this said, take up your shield of faith so you will be protected from Lucifer's well-aimed fiery darts and be able to advance in the midst of the battle. Let Him be pleased with your words as you say it in strength: *"I am able to walk by faith and not by sight."*

Never forget that the King is always protecting you. Grab hold of your shield of faith and boldly proclaim it: *"I am protected by the King."*

Keep in mind that He hides you in the shadow of His wings. He is a shield around you. In view of this wonderful truth, know that you are hidden in the King's Son, the Prince of Peace. Whisper it: *"I am hidden in Him."*

Until I can find a way to get my next letter to you on the battlefield, always remember to take up your shield of faith.

Walking by faith,
Your Protected Servant

Chapter Sixteen

Crowned with the Helmet of Victory

You Are Crowned in Victory

Therefore, prepare your minds for action;
be self-controlled;
set your hope fully on the grace to be given you
when Jesus Christ is revealed.
1 Peter 1:13

$\mathcal{D}$ear Beloved Believer,

In this letter, I want to tell you about the helmet of victory that you have been given. As you know, you were victorious in your struggle against Lucifer, the deceiver, the moment you accepted the King's offer of salvation—for salvation means victory. You were triumphant the instant you accepted the Prince of Peace as your Lord and Savior! Now the King desires you to *walk in that victory* each day. He desires you to be equipped and ready for battle at all times, for, as you know, your enemy prowls around like a roaring lion looking for someone to devour. Do not let that someone be you!

Let's look once again at Paul's words in the book of Ephesians:

Finally, my brethren, be strong in the Lord and in the power of His might. Put on the whole armor of God,

155

that you may be able to stand against the wiles of
[Lucifer] the devil. . . . And take the helmet of salvation.
—Ephesians 6:10-11,17a, NKJV

In war, one of the most sought-after targets is the head.
If a soldier is wounded in this area, he will most likely die.
In Paul's day, the enemies of Rome employed a frightful
weapon called the broad sword to strike at the Roman soldiers' heads. The blade of this sword measured about three
to four feet in length and was supported by a large handle.
Unlike the thin fencing swords the Three Musketeers used,
the broad sword could only be wielded with two hands, and
its weight required the soldier to hold it like a baseball bat.
It was designed to be brought down on the opponent's *head*,
striking and slicing his skull in two.

Faced with the power of this awesome weapon, the Roman soldier needed a rugged helmet to protect his head and
give him confidence in battle. For this reason, the high-
ranking soldiers wore helmets made of cast-metal, while
the lesser-ranking soldiers wore helmets made of leather
trimmed with metal. The soldier would carry this helmet
over his shoulder or strap it to his belt so it would be at hand
in case of a surprise attack. The soldier knew his helmet was
of the utmost importance because it protected his mind, so
he kept it accessible at all times.

Just like the enemies who wielded broad swords against
the Romans, Lucifer and his cohorts will employ fearsome
weapons against you. They will seek to divide your mind
through the weapon of deceit. They will attempt to land a
decisive blow to discourage you and cause you to doubt the
King. In view of this, you must always be equipped with
the helmet of salvation, for the only way to have victory is
to protect your mind. Remember that you are called to have
the mind of the Prince of Peace.

It is important to understand that when you accepted the King's offer to join His family, you were not called to turn off your mind or your intellect. You need to study the King's Word each day, for if you do not, your relationship with the King will suffer and Lucifer, the deceiver, will have an easier time trying to lead you astray. Just as Paul instructed the Corinthians, you must be careful not to let the enemy attack your mind:

> I am afraid that just as Eve was deceived by the serpent's cunning, your minds may somehow be led astray from your sincere and pure devotion to Christ. For if someone comes to you and preaches a Jesus other than the Jesus we preached, or if you receive a different spirit from the one you received, or a different gospel from the one you accepted, you put up with it easily enough.
>
> —2 Corinthians 11:3-4a

When Paul told the Corinthians they had "put up" with these things easily enough, he meant they had lost their discernment and had become tolerant of the deceivers in their midst. They had accepted a Jesus other than the Prince of Peace, the King's one and only Son, and had believed in a gospel other than the one Paul had preached. He had similar words for the believers in Galatia:

> I am astonished that you are so quickly deserting the one who called you by the grace of Christ and are turning to a different gospel—which is really no gospel at all. Evidently some people are throwing you into confusion and are trying to pervert the gospel of Christ. But even if we or an angel from heaven should preach a gospel other than the one we preached to you, let him be eternally condemned! As we have already said, so now I say again: If anybody is preaching to

you a gospel other than what you accepted, let him
be eternally condemned!

—Galatians 1:6-9

Lucifer will use these tactics of deceit to divide your
mind and cause you to doubt the King. He will try to per-
vert the true gospel of Jesus Christ, the Prince of Peace, and
convince you to follow a false way. It is a tactic that he has
been using since the Garden of Eden, when he successfully deceived Eve and led her and Adam astray. Let's look at
three ways he was able to infiltrate Adam and Eve's minds
and plant seeds of doubt against the King.

First, Lucifer approached Eve and *questioned* the word of
the King, which caused her to doubt the King's *truth*. Look at
how he placed doubt in Eve's mind with his twisted words:

> Now the serpent was more crafty than any of the wild
> animals the LORD God had made. He said to the
> woman, "Did God really say, 'You must not eat from
> any tree in the garden'?"
>
> —Genesis 3:1

Once Lucifer had caused Eve to doubt, he went on to
deny what the King had said to her. The King had clearly
told Adam and Eve, "You are free to eat from any tree in the
garden; but you must not eat from the tree of the knowledge
of good and evil, for when you eat of it you will surely die"
(Genesis 2:16-17). But Lucifer cunningly denied this, saying
to Eve, "You will not surely die" (Genesis 3:4). Lucifer then
completed his assault by *substituting* his own lie in place of
the King's Word. Listen to what he had to say: "For God
knows that when you eat of it your eyes will be opened, and
you will be like God, knowing good and evil" (Genesis 3:5).

Lucifer has been weaving his twisted lies ever since to
divide people's minds and separate them from the King.
Look at how he worked in Simon Peter's life. One day, the

Prince of Peace asked His disciples, "Who do people say that the Son of Man is?" (Matthew 16:13, ESV). Simon Peter answered, "You are the Christ, the Son of the living God" (Matthew 16:16, ESV). Peter was equipped with his helmet of salvation and was walking in victory. But then the Prince of Peace told His disciples that He was about to suffer and be killed. When Peter heard this, he took off his helmet and allowed Lucifer to deceive his mind. As the scribe Matthew relates:

> From that time Jesus began to show his disciples that he must go to Jerusalem and suffer many things from the elders and chief priests and scribes, and be killed, and on the third day be raised. Peter took him aside and began to rebuke him, saying, "Far be it from you, Lord! This shall never happen to you." But he turned and said to Peter, "Get behind me, Satan! You are a hindrance to me. *For you are not setting your mind on the things of God*, but on the things of man."
> —Matthew 16:21-23, ESV, emphasis added

Lucifer knew just what fiery dart to aim at Peter's thoughts to split his mind in two. Peter did not want to see the Prince of Peace killed, so he set his mind on the things of men and not the things of the King. At that moment he did not have the mind of Christ, and because of this, he did not have on his helmet of salvation. Lucifer's skillfully brandished sword of deception found its target, and Peter became a hindrance to the King's plan and the purpose for which the Prince of Peace had come to the world.

You can also hinder the work of the King when you set your mind on your own desires and wishes and not the purposes of the Prince of Peace. You must always beware, for Lucifer, the schemer, will use these age-old tactics of warfare to divide your mind. He will cause you to *question* the Word of the King by placing doubt in your thoughts. He will *deny* the Word of the King by convincing you that what the King has said to you is not true. He will then twist the Word of the King through deceit and *substitute* it with his own lies. This is why you must always have the mind of Christ, the Prince of Peace, and set your mind on the things of the King. When you do, Lucifer will not be able to target you with his well-woven lies.

But what exactly does it mean to have the "mind of Christ"? According to Warren Wiersbe, "To 'have the mind of Christ' means to look at life from the Savior's point of view, having his values and desires in mind. It means to think God's thoughts and not think as the world thinks."[1] When you have the mind of Christ, your thoughts are focused on the King and you are protected from the onslaught of Lucifer, the deceiver. This is what it means to be equipped with the helmet of salvation—to have a mind that is totally devoted to the King of kings.

In a previous letter, I stated that you are to be an imitator of the King. This means that you are to imitate the *thoughts* of the King. But what are those thoughts? Look at what one of the King's prophets wrote, speaking on the King's behalf:

> Can a mother forget the baby at her breast and have no compassion on the child she has borne? Though she may forget, I will not forget you! See, I have engraved you on the palms of my hands; your walls are ever before me.
>
> —Isaiah 49:15-16

You are always in the King's thoughts! With this in mind, be His imitator and set your mind on the *things of the King* by continually thinking of Him. As Paul wrote, "Your attitude should be the same as that of Christ Jesus" (Philippians 2:5).

This means putting on your helmet of salvation and keeping the King in your thoughts every moment of the day. It means always thinking, *What would the King have me do in this situation? Does it line up with His Word?* Then, when Lucifer and his cohorts try to shoot a fiery dart of doubt into your mind, you will be able to look to the truth of who the King is and discern right from wrong.

Always remember, beloved believer, that you are in the King's thoughts. Consider the depth of His love as you exclaim, *"I am always in the King's thoughts."*

In view of this love, put on your helmet of salvation and know that you are called to have the mind of Christ. Say it out loud: *"I am called to have the mind of Christ, the Prince of Peace."*

By having the mind of Christ, you will be able to discern right from wrong—the truth from the lies—which will enable you to walk in victory. Move forward in battle as you declare, *"I am able to walk in victory!"*

You are crowned in victory. Shout it for all to hear: *"I am crowned in victory!"*

Until I can write again, keep your helmet of salvation firmly in place and protect yourself from Lucifer's attacks by placing your thoughts on the King.

Putting on the mind of Christ,

Your Undivided Servant

Chapter Seventeen

Crowned in Holiness

You Are Set Apart

*To those sanctified in Christ Jesus
and called to be holy. . . .
Put on the new self,
created to be like God in true righteousness and holiness.*
1 Corinthians 1:2b; Ephesians 4:24

Dear Beloved Believer,

Now that you know about the helmet of salvation and have learned to walk in victory, it is time for me to tell you about another crown that was placed on your head at the moment of your salvation. As the scribe Ezekiel has written, when you joined the King's family, He *dressed you in fine linen, adorned you with jewelry,* and also put *a beautiful crown on your head* (see Ezekiel 16:10-12). However, with this crown comes a certain amount of responsibility. Allow me to explain.

Recently, I read a story about the life of Queen Victoria. She was England's longest-ruling monarch. She became queen when she was only 18 years old and ruled for 64 years. As the account I read stated:

> When she was young, Victoria was shielded from the fact that she would be the next ruling monarch of England lest this knowledge spoil her. When her

teacher finally did let her discover for herself that she would one day be Queen of England, Victoria's response was, "Then I will be good!" Her life would be controlled by her position. No matter where she was, Victoria was governed by the fact that she sat on the throne of England.[1]

From the moment Victoria discovered the truth of who she was—the next queen of England—she determined in her heart and mind to be good. She determined to walk worthy of her calling. In the same way, I would like to help you discover who you are in Christ—the King's Son, the Prince of Peace—and how to walk worthy of that calling. For you are betrothed to the Prince of Peace, and because of this, you have been set apart for Him. This is the reason people are watching you. In view of this, I pray that you will declare as Queen Victoria did, "Then I will be good!"

Now, before I explain how you have been set apart, there is another interesting point that I first want you to consider. Throughout my letters, I have quoted many times from the apostle Paul, a scribe of the King. Each of these writings I quoted was originally a letter drafted from Paul to a community of believers in a specific place (such as Rome, Ephesus, Philippi and so forth). Not only that, but Paul always addressed these letters to the *saints* in these communities.

Unfortunately, today there is some confusion over the meaning of the word "saints." Many believe that saints are people who have died and have achieved a special level of spiritual eminence. However, as Warren Wiersbe notes:

> No word in the New Testament has suffered more than this word *saint*. Even the dictionary defines a *saint* as a "person officially recognized for holiness of life." Who makes this official recognition? Usually some religious body, and the process by which a person becomes a

saint is technically known as *canonization*. The deceased person's life is examined carefully to see whether he qualifies for sainthood. If the candidate's character and conduct are found to be above reproach, if he has been responsible for working at least two miracles, then he is qualified to be made a saint. As interesting as this procedure is, we do not find it authorized in the Bible.[2]

In the book of Ephesians, Paul addresses his readers as "saints" on nine separate occasions. These saints were *alive*—not dead—though at one time each had been dead in their transgressions and sins. It is also clear that these people *never performed any miracles,* though they did experience a miracle the moment they trusted the King's Son as their Lord and Savior. In the same way, from the moment you were clothed in the garments of salvation, *you* became a saint. As the King's Word declares:

> You are no longer strangers and foreigners, but fellow citizens with the saints and the members of the household of God.
>
> —Ephesians 2:19b, NKJV

Wiersbe goes onto say, "The word *saint* means 'one who has been set apart.' It is related to the word *sanctified*, which [also] means 'set apart.'"[3] The definition of "saint" can also refer to a person who is "free from sin,"[4] and the definition of "sanctity" means "holiness of life and character."[5] "Sanctification" is actually an ongoing process that refers "to the practice of godliness in the life of a believer, and especially to the process by which a person who has been saved progresses toward the goal of becoming like God and Christ."[6] To put it in a nutshell, you are a *saint* since you have been set apart by the King of kings to live a life of holiness as you become more like the Prince of Peace. This is why the King's Word teaches,

"Make every effort to live in peace with all men and to be holy; without holiness no one will see the Lord" (Hebrews 12:14).

In a previous letter, I stated that righteousness is both a *one-time event* (you receive *positional righteousness* at the moment of your salvation) and an *ongoing process* (you engage in *practical righteousness* throughout your life). In the same way, there is a practical aspect of sanctification that you must live out each day. Look again at the story of Queen Victoria's life. Because of her royal birth, she knew that she would one day be the future queen of England. This was the *positional aspect* of her monarchy—the moment she was born, she was immediately in line to rule the country. The practical aspect of her rule occurred when she learned she would be queen and declared, "Then I will be good!" From that moment on, she determined to be the person that her birth and position had called her to be. She began the *ongoing process* of conducting her life in the way a queen should.

The same is true of your practical sanctification. Because of who you are in Christ, you are called to be holy and set apart for the King. Like Queen Victoria, you are to determine in your heart and your mind that you will be good, for this is what will differentiate you from others. People are observing your life, and as they see you reflect the King's glory, they will be drawn to Him. Remember that this is one of the reasons why you were given life!

As a child of the King, you are *called to be holy and called to be a saint* (see 1 Corinthians 1:2b; Romans 1:7a). This is an ongoing process that can only be achieved by walking in the way of holiness. As the scribe Isaiah writes:

> And a highway will be there; it will be called the Way of Holiness. . . . It will be for those who walk in that Way; wicked fools will not go about on it.
>
> —Isaiah 35:8

As I have said, the word "holiness" in Hebrew means to be set apart for God.[7] The word "way" in Hebrew not only means journey or direction but also "course of life" and "of moral character."[8] Therefore, when you *walk in the way of holiness*, you embark on a journey of moral character and live in such a way that you are set apart from the things of this world. The *Blue Letter Bible* states it this way: "It is a way by itself, distinguished from the way of the world, for it is a way of separation from, and nonconformity to, this world. It shall be for those whom the Lord has set apart for himself."[9] This is the duty of every saint: to live a life of holiness.

On June 20, 1837, when Victoria was told that her uncle, King William IV, had died and that she was now queen of England, she wrote in her journal, "Since it has pleased Providence to place me in this station, I shall do my utmost to fulfill my duty towards my country."[10] Because of her position, Victoria was willing to offer herself as a living sacrifice for her nation. The same must be true of you. Look at what Paul writes:

> Therefore, I urge you, brothers, in view of God's mercy, to offer your bodies as living sacrifices, holy and pleasing to God—this is your spiritual act of worship. Do not conform any longer to the pattern of this world, but be transformed by the renewing of your mind. Then you will be able to test and approve what God's will is—his good, pleasing and perfect will.
>
> —Romans 12:1-2

Because of who you are—your position in Christ, the Prince of Peace—you are called to offer your body as a living sacrifice, holy and pleasing to your King, for this is your spiritual act of worship. By offering yourself in this way—by declaring to be good—you can no longer conform to the pattern of this world. In view of this, as you determine in your heart to be set apart, you must exclude those things from your life that do not contribute to the King's work of renewing of your mind. Again, the crown you have been given carries with it a certain amount of responsibility. This is where that responsibility comes into play, for there are two aspects to sanctification: the putting off of evil and the putting on of good.

The King's Word calls you to put off evil practices, shun sexual immorality (including lustful thoughts), cast off deceitful desires, and rid yourself of anger, rage, bitterness, malice, stealing, slander and even filthy language. You are called to "throw off everything that hinders and the sin that so easily entangles" (Hebrews 12:1b). In place of these things, you are to put on "your new self" so that you can be like the King in true righteousness and holiness. Note what Paul writes:

> You were taught, with regard to your former way of life, *to put off your old self,* which is being corrupted by its deceitful desires; to be made new in the attitude of your minds; and *to put on the new self,* created to be like God in true righteousness and holiness.
> —Ephesians 4:22-24, emphasis added

As you know, you are standing in the middle of an unseen battlefield, and on your own you do not have the power to do good in the sight of the King. So, how do you achieve what the King is commanding you to do? How do you put off the old self and put on the new so you can achieve practical sanctification? The key is to tap into the power of the Royal Counselor, the Holy Spirit, who is already at work within you (see Ephesians 3:20). He has crowned you and given you the strength to live a life holy and pleasing to your King, regardless of how fierce the battle rages around you.

In fact, in the Hebrew, the word for "crown" (*atarah*) also means to encircle as in war.[11] This is exactly what the Royal Counselors does—He encircles you and empowers you to put on the new and do what is right.

As I conclude this letter, I want you to remember that it is the King who has set you apart, and it is He who will give you the strength to walk in the way of holiness. Another name of the King is Jehovah-Mekaddishkem, "the Lord who Sanctifies." In view of this, move the truth of who you are from your head to your heart and begin to make choices based on that truth. Then, with all authority, rightfully claim your inheritance as you shout out loud, *"I am a saint!"*

Remember that you have been set apart to reflect the King's glory. Ponder with wonder: *"I am set apart."*

You are also a member of the King's household. Hold you head high as you accept how special this is and say, *"I am a member of the King's household."*

You are royalty! State it with grandeur: *"I am royalty!"*

You are called to be holy. Whisper it in reverence: *"I am called to be holy."*

By the power and strength of the Royal Counselor, you are able to walk in the way of holiness. Walk directly and circumspectly as you assert, *"I am able to walk in the way of holiness."*

You have been crowned in holiness. So, with regal authority, reply, *"I am crowned in holiness."*

In fact, because of who you are in Christ, the Prince of Peace, you are righteous and holy. Cherish this truth in the depths of your heart as you embrace it: *"I am righteous and holy because of who I am in Christ, the King's Son."*

Soon I will find a way to get my next letter to you, for there is a refining process taking place in your life that I need to tell you more about. Until then, hold your head high and walk in the manner worthy of who you are in the King's Son, the Prince of Peace.

Walking in the way of holiness,
Your Crowned Servant

Chapter Eighteen

Adorned with Gold and Silver

You Are Refined by the Fire

In this you greatly rejoice, though now for a little while
you may have had to suffer grief in all kinds of trials.
These have come so that your faith—of greater worth than gold,
which perishes even though refined by fire—
may be proved genuine and may result in praise,
glory and honor when Jesus Christ is revealed.
1 Peter 1:6-7

$\mathcal{D}$ear Beloved Believer,

In the passage that we have been studying from Ezekiel, he states that the King has not only placed a beautiful crown on your head but has also *adorned you with gold and silver* (see Ezekiel 16:13a). As you know, gold and silver reflect light, which is why they glimmer and shine in the sun. In the same way, the King wants you to reflect His light so you can shine to those around you. However, to do that, you will often have to go through the *refiner's fire.*

The best way to understand what I mean by this is to study the way that gold and silver are refined. When the craftsman desires to perfect the metal—to bring it to its purest form—he heats it to an intense temperature. This reduces the gold or silver to a fluid state. The craftsman then adds a solvent, such as alkali or lead, which combines with the melted metal. When the craftsman raises the temperature, the solvent brings the impurities of the gold or silver to the top. This impurity is called the "dross."

Note that the craftsman is present and watching at all times for just the precise moment to pour off the dross, or the impurities. Once he does so, he will again heat the liquid to an intense temperature, which will raise more impurities to the surface. He repeats this process again and again until he can look down on the gold or silver and see his own reflection in the molten liquid. At this point—and *only* at this point—will he consider the gold to be in its purest form and the purification process to be complete. When the metal is absolutely pure, it is ready to be transformed into his creations and works of art.

The same is true of the refining process that Jehovah-Hoseenu, "the Lord Our Maker," performs in your life. Your King is the Master Craftsman, and the Word teaches that He is a consuming fire (see Hebrews 12:29). He is known as the Refiner (see Malachi 3:3), and He uses His refining fire to continue to sanctify you and remove all of the impurities from your life. As the King said through the scribe Isaiah:

> I will turn my hand against you; I will thoroughly purge away your dross and remove all your impurities.
>
> —Isaiah 1:25

When I first read the King's words in this passage, I had trouble comprehending why He would say such a thing. If He truly loves us deeply, why would He turn His hand against us to purge our impurities? But then I read these words from Peter, which explained everything:

> These have come so that your faith—of greater worth than gold, which perishes even though refined by

fire—may be proved genuine and may result in praise,
glory and honor when Jesus Christ is revealed.

—1 Peter 1:7

There are two wonderful reasons why the King of kings
desires to remove the impurities in your life. The first is so
that *"your faith . . . may be proved genuine."* As the *Blue Letter
Bible* states, "Our faith isn't tested because God is ignorant
of its nature or quality, but because we often are ignorant
of it—God's purpose in testing is to display the enduring
quality of our faith."[1] When you are put through the fire,
your faith comes out stronger—for deep within your heart
you are more fully convinced of who the King of kings is
and the depth of His love for you. As a result, you become
more like the precious Prince of Peace.

This brings us to the second reason why the King desires
to refine you. As a believer, you have been given the name
"Christian." This name means to be Christlike. Although
many fall short of this name, the King desires you to become Christlike so that, once again, *you can reflect His glory
to everyone watching.* When you go through the refiner's fire,
the impurities—the dross—will surface and be removed so
that your faith will be proved genuine and become real deep
within your heart. As a result, praise, glory and honor will
be given to the One who deserves it.

Let me explain how this works. When the King allows
you to go through trials and difficulties, it causes you to examine your faith and your trust in the King. If you choose
to stand firm and to hold fast to Him as the temperature
rises, and if you allow Him to do His work, then you will
come out of the time of difficulty with a stronger faith than
when you went in. As a result, those around you who are
watching as you experience these trials will notice there is
something different about you—that you are drawing from

a strength that is not your own. In this way, your life will serve as a reflection of the King's glory, and others will see the treasure you hold inside.

Always take comfort in the fact that the Master Craftsman is present during any trial and that He has His hand on the thermostat. He will allow the refining process to continue until He can look down upon your life in love and see His reflection in you. At that point, He will be satisfied that the deep heart work has been done within you, and Paul's words in 2 Corinthians 3:18 will become real in your life:

> And we, who with unveiled faces all reflect the Lord's glory, are being transformed into his likeness with ever-increasing glory, which comes from the Lord who is the Spirit.

It is for this reason that the scribe James wrote, "Consider it pure joy, my brothers, whenever you face trials of many kinds, because you know that the testing of your faith develops perseverance. *Perseverance must finish its work so that you may be mature and complete, not lacking anything*" (James 1:2-4, emphasis added). I know that this seems a difficult prospect, but it is the truth. Because of the deep love the King has for you, He will use suffering as a tool to mold you into the person He wants you to be and make you mature and complete.

The King knows how to balance the events in your life. If you only experienced blessings, you would become proud and believe you had no need for the King. So, the King allows you to experience trials, difficulties and suffering to remove impurities like pride and self-sufficiency and draw you closer to Him. For this reason, as James states, you should not be discouraged when you encounter suffering but "consider it pure joy."

Think about the life of the apostle Paul for a moment. We know that the King deeply loved Paul, and that He used Paul mightily for His Kingdom. So why then did the King allow a physical trial in Paul's life? How could suffering possibly benefit Paul when he had so much work to do for the King? One of the reasons becomes obvious when you read Paul's words in 2 Corinthians 12:7-10:

> To keep me from becoming conceited because of these surpassingly great revelations, there was given me a thorn in my flesh, a messenger of Satan, to torment me. Three times I pleaded with the Lord to take it away from me. But he said to me, "My grace is sufficient for you, for my power is made perfect in weakness." Therefore I will boast all the more gladly about my weaknesses, so that Christ's power may rest on me. That is why, for Christ's sake, I delight in weaknesses, in insults, in hardships, in persecutions, in difficulties. For when I am weak, then I am strong.

The hardship Paul faced *kept him from becoming conceited*. The King knew the deep heart impurities in Paul, just as He knows the deep heart impurities in you. So, He allowed trials, difficulties and suffering to occur in Paul's life as a means of purifying and sanctifying him. When Paul was humbled and weakened by these difficulties, he experienced the King's grace and became strong. The same is true of you. The King wants you to be all that He created you to be, and He will not allow any impurity to keep His will from being fulfilled in your life.

In Paul's case, the King used a physical trial. As Warren Wiersbe writes, "We do not know what Paul's thorn in the flesh was. The word translated *thorn* means 'a sharp stake used for torturing or impaling someone.' It was a physical affliction of some kind that brought pain and distress to Paul.

Some Bible students think that Paul had an eye affliction (see Galatians 6:11); but we cannot know for sure. It is a good thing that we do not know, because no matter what our sufferings may be, we are able to apply the lessons Paul learned to get encouragement."[2]

Notice in the above passage that Paul states, "There was given me a thorn in my flesh, a messenger of Satan, to torment me." As Wiersbe goes onto say, the word "torment" means "'to beat, to strike with a fist.' The tense of the verb indicates that this pain was either constant or recurring."[3] In other words, the thorn in Paul's flesh was a terrible affliction that caused constant or recurring pain. It was so distressing that Paul pleaded *three times* with the King to take it away. Interesting! Remember that in the Garden of Gethsemane, your Prince of Peace also pleaded three times with the King to not be made to suffer. Yet, like Paul, He was so in tune with the King that He knew the suffering was necessary. It was the only way to fulfill the King's plan, and so He prayed, "Yet not my will, but yours be done" (Luke 22:42b).

There is nothing wrong with coming to the King and asking to be healed. Many times, He chooses to heal as a means to glorify Himself—but not every time. Sometimes, as in Paul's case, He will say, "My grace is sufficient for you, for my power is made perfect in weakness" (2 Corinthians 12:9b). In these situations, you must be willing to listen to His answer and accept it, for you never know when the King is using the difficulty to bring about a greater plan. This was certainly true of Paul's life. Others were watching his life and observing how he dealt with suffering, and as they saw him persevere, it pointed them to the King. Look again at what Paul wrote:

> Therefore I will boast all the more gladly about my
> weaknesses, so that Christ's power may rest on me.

That is why, for Christ's sake, I delight in weaknesses,
in insults, in hardships, in persecutions, in difficulties.
For when I am weak, then I am strong.
—2 Corinthians 12:9c-10

If we desire to be Christlike, we can also learn from the suffering we find in Christ's life. We too can boast and rejoice in knowing that we are adorned with gold and silver in the midst of the trials, difficulties and suffering. We too can say, "And we rejoice in the hope of the glory of God. Not only so, but we also rejoice in our sufferings, because we know that suffering produces perseverance" (Romans 5:2b-3). We *are* able to persevere in the midst of the fire, and the King *will* fulfill His purpose in our lives as we walk in the midst of the trouble.

In view of the marvelous glory you reflect, let the King hear you say, *"I am not discouraged by suffering."*

When you are weak and hold on to the King of kings, you will experience a strength that is not your own. When this takes place, you can join with the apostle Paul on the front lines of the battle and claim, *"When I am weak, then I am strong."*

For with the power available to you through the power of the Royal Counselor, you can declare, *"I am able to persevere!"*

As you rely on this strength and power in the midst of the fire, you can walk forward and state, *"I am able to walk in the midst of trouble."*

The King refines you by fire so you can be pure and reflect His beauty. As you go through the refining process, may others be drawn to the light within you as you glowingly announce, *"I am refined by the fire."*

Never forget that you are adorned in gold and silver. Shine brightly and exclaim, *"I am adorned with gold and silver."*

Continue to persevere and shine for the King no matter what comes your way. Soon, I will find a way to get my next letter to you so that you can be prepared to go on the offensive and fight the good fight.

Being purified by the fire,

Your Refined Servant

Chapter Nineteen

Equipped with the Sword of the Spirit

You Are Able to Fight the Good Fight

*For the word of God is living and active,
sharper than any two-edged sword,
piercing to the division of soul and of spirit, of joints and of marrow,
and discerning the thoughts and intentions of the heart.*
Hebrews 4:12, ESV

*D*ear Beloved Believer,

Up until now, I have taught you how to defend yourself in battle. Now, it is time to pick up your weapon and take the fight to Lucifer, your enemy. Just as every military soldier learns both defensive and offensive modes of attack, you must learn how to not only stand your ground but also launch an offensive assault against Lucifer, your foe. With this in mind, it is time to learn how to rightly divide the Word of the King.

As you know, the King has provided you with defensive armor to protect you from the attacks and tactics of Lucifer. These include the belt of truth, the breastplate of righteousness, the sandals of peace, the shield of faith and the helmet of salvation. But the King has also provided you with offensive weapons that you can use to skillfully attack and destroy Lucifer and his many cohorts. These weapons include the sword of the Spirit and prayer. In this letter, I will focus on training you how to use the sword of the Spirit so you can wield it effectively in battle.

As Paul writes, you are to "be strong in the Lord and in the power of His might" and take up "the sword of the Spirit, which is the word of God" (Ephesians 6:10b,17, NKJV). In Paul's day, soldiers had two kinds of swords. One was the broad sword, which, if you remember, was large and heavy. The soldier would brandish this sword with two hands and attempt to slice his opponent's head in two. The second sword that the Roman soldiers used, called the *machaira*, was much smaller. Roman soldiers kept this sword nestled in a case strapped to their belt at all times. This is the sword that the apostle Paul termed "the sword of the Spirit," which is the Word of God.

The *machaira* was approximately 6 to 18 inches in length and was specifically used for hand-to-hand combat. To be effective in battle, the soldier had to know how to handle it skillfully. The same is true for you—you must be trained to use your sword skillfully to fight the good fight and bring glory and honor to the King of kings. Remember what the apostle Paul wrote:

> For though we live in the world, we do not wage war as the world does. The weapons we fight with are not the weapons of the world. On the contrary, they have divine power to demolish stronghold. We demolish arguments and every pretension that sets itself up against the knowledge of God, and we take captive every thought to make it obedient to Christ.
>
> —2 Corinthians 10:3-5

In addition to taking your thoughts captive and making them obedient to the Prince of Peace, it is also important for you to demolish any and every argument that sets itself up against the knowledge of the King. Lucifer, the liar, has set up many arguments and pretentions that have caused confusion within the Kingdom. In using the sword of the Spirit as an offensive weapon, it is the Word of God that will give you knowledge of the King. It will give you discernment so you can smash down any argument that comes against that knowledge before problems arise.

There are actually two different Greek words used in the New Testament to describe the Word: *logos* and *rhema*. *Logos* speaks of the general Word of the King, which is what the belt of truth represents. *Rhema*, on the other hand, speaks of specific words or statements from the Word. As Danny Bond explains, "*Rhema* is the piercing double-edged sword that defines specific truths to the child of God, allowing him to apply these truths to temptations and situations where [Lucifer] attempts to attack him."[1] Here is how the author of Hebrews describes it:

> For the word of God is living and active, sharper than any two-edged sword, piercing to the division of soul and of spirit, of joints and of marrow, and discerning the thoughts and intentions of the heart. And no creature is hidden from his sight, but all are naked and exposed to the eyes of him to whom we must give account.
>
> —Hebrews 4:12-13

Lucifer, the schemer, knows the King's Word better than you and me, and many times he twists it to deceive people. He studies it and memorizes it, and then he corrupts it to cause people to stumble and fall through false teachings. Remember that he used these tactics in the Garden of Eden to cause Adam and Eve to stumble, and he tried to use them against the Prince of Peace Himself.

If you do not learn how to wield your sword properly, Lucifer will grab it right out of your hand and stab you in the back with it. For this reason, you must understand what the Word truly says and be ready to use it to demolish any stronghold the enemy attempts to set up against you. Then, and only then, will you be able to go on the offensive, slicing apart the lies of the enemy before they hit their target. In time, you will find that you will even be able to use your sword to cut out any lies that have *hit their target*, thus preventing the enemy's fiery darts from catching hold and burning out of control. However, this can only happen if you have been trained to effectively wield your sword of the Spirit.

You will receive this training in two ways. The first is to find a teaching pastor who can equip you with the Word of the King. However, as Bond notes, you must be cautious, for "the sword of the Spirit is sharp. Nothing cuts cleaner and deeper on the face of the earth. To become skillful with the sword of the Spirit, we must go to a church where specific biblical truths are taught. Many ministers and many philosophies exist, especially in the day and age in which we live, that do not abide in the Word of God."[2]

With this in mind, do not choose a church or gathering of believers based on unimportant things such as tradition, location, or the fact that the church has a nice building. Instead, choose a place of worship where you will be fully trained in how to handle your sword. You need to be able to walk in strength so you can be all the King created you to be, bring glory and honor to Him, and lead a life that impacts others. Seek out a church that teaches the Word of God verse by verse and chapter by chapter so that Lucifer cannot deceive you by twisting it.

A second way to be trained in wielding your sword is by reading it and studying it on a daily basis. As Paul writes,

"Be diligent to present yourself approved to God, a worker who does not need to be ashamed, rightly dividing the word of truth" (2 Timothy 2:15, NKJV). Bond further explains, "By devoting yourself to careful study of the Word, comparing Scripture to Scripture, you equip yourself to discern what is solid doctrine."[3]

Remember that just as the Roman soldier kept his sword strapped to his leather belt, you must keep the sword of the Spirit strapped to your belt of truth at all times so you can be equipped for every good work the King has for you. When you have your sword at the ready, you will be able to advance forward in battle, rightly dividing the lies from the truth. You will be able to overcome Lucifer, the father of lies, and his many schemes. As the King's Word declares:

> All Scripture is God-breathed and is useful for teaching, rebuking, correcting and training in righteousness, so that the man of God may be thoroughly equipped for every good work.
>
> —2 Timothy 3:16-17

As you train in using your sword, you must be like the believers in Berea, who searched the Word daily. As Luke tells us, "The Bereans were of more noble character than the Thessalonians, for they received the message with great eagerness and examined the Scriptures every day to see if what Paul said was true" (Acts 17:11). The Bereans didn't immediately accept what Paul had taught them and assume it to be true, but instead searched out the Scriptures for confirmation. Likewise, you must compare Scripture to Scripture to make sure what you are being taught is true.

It is important for you to make sure that what you are hearing is not false doctrine. Don't just believe what someone says because he or she seems to have a lot of knowledge or has an impressive-sounding title, or because everyone seems to be following him or her. Many times the lies you hear will sound convincing, because the false teachers will use the King's Word out of context. They will extract a verse or two and use their own interpretation to explain the meaning. Even well-meaning children of the King will continue to spread the lie, because they are not like the Bereans who searched the Scriptures daily.

You can defend against falling into this same trap by being prepared and searching the Word daily to discern the truth. As Paul wrote, you must "do your best to present yourself to God as one approved, a workman who does not need to be ashamed and *who correctly handles the word of truth*" (2 Timothy 2:15, emphasis added). When you do this, you will be able to fight from an offensive position on the frontlines, in hand-to-hand combat, against Lucifer and his many cohorts.

With all this said, join with your fellow believers and take the battle to your enemy. As the psalmist wrote, "Let the high praises of God be in their mouth, and a two-edged sword in their hand" (Psalm 149:6, NKJV). You are able to fight the good fight, so let the King hear you shout it: *"I am able to fight the good fight!"*

You have been trained to rightly divide the Word of the King. Slice it out loud, *"I am able to rightly divide the Word of the King."*

In view of this marvelous truth, rejoice as you say, *"I am able to overcome Lucifer, the devil."*

You are thoroughly equipped for every good work. Stand tall as you declare, *"I am thoroughly equipped for every good work."*

Move forward in your walk with the King, for you are able to walk in strength. Say it strong: *"I am able to walk in strength."*

Until the next letter arrives, stand firm as you rightly divide the Word of the King with the sword of the Spirit.

Slicing apart the lies,
Your Well-Equipped Fellow Soldier

Chapter Twenty

Clothed in Unfading Beauty

You Are a Partaker of His Divine Nature

Make every effort to supplement your faith with virtue,
and virtue with knowledge, and knowledge with self-control,
and self-control with steadfastness, and steadfastness with godliness,
and godliness with brotherly affection, and brotherly affection with love.
For if these qualities are yours and are increasing,
they keep you from being ineffective or unfruitful
in the knowledge of our Lord Jesus Christ.
2 Peter 1:5-8, ESV

*D*ear Beloved Believer,

In this letter, I want to share with you the greatest beauty treatment ever passed down from generation to generation to those loved by the King. Unlike the empty remedies we find on the market today—remedies that give external short-term results—this treatment will give you long-term *unfading* beauty on the inside. It will bring love, compassion and contentment into your life. As the scribe Peter writes:

> Your beauty should not come from outward adornment, such as braided hair and the wearing of gold jewelry and fine clothes. Instead, it should be that of your inner self, the unfading beauty of a gentle and quiet spirit, which is of great worth in God's sight.
>
> —1 Peter 3:3-4

This *unfading* beauty treatment will result in a gentle and quiet spirit, which is beautiful indeed and is of great worth in the King's sight. However, to receive it, you must follow the King's special diet so you can nourish your innermost being. Ezekiel describes this diet in the passage we have been studying:

> Your food was fine flour, honey and olive oil. You became very beautiful and rose to be a queen.
>
> —Ezekiel 16:13

Have you ever looked into the eyes of someone who is starving physically and seen the depth of that person's despair? There is no warmth, glow or light in that person's eyes—only hopelessness and despair. The same is true of those who are starving spiritually. Although they may possess great outer beauty, if you look deep into their eyes, you will find no warmth, no glow and no light—only hopelessness and despair. These individuals may have feasted on the best food money can buy, but they did not feast on the healthiest and most satisfying food offered by the King. As a result, they do not possess the unfading beauty that the King truly values. To protect yourself, you must consume the King's special diet of "fine flour," "honey" and "olive oil." Let's look at each of these items in turn.

First, when you read about *fine flour* in the book of Ezekiel, it should bring to mind the Prince of Peace, who is also known as the Bread of Life (see John 6:35). As you know, the Bible is the *written* Word of the King. But there is also a *living* Word. Look at what John writes:

> In the beginning was the Word, and the Word was with God, and the Word was God. . . . The Word became flesh and made his dwelling among us.
>
> —John 1:1,14a

The Living Word is the *Prince of Peace Himself,* and He is inseparably bound together with the written Word. Why? Because the written Word, the Bible, is a *snapshot* of the Living Word, while the Living Word, the Prince of Peace, is the *embodiment* of the written Word. The written Word tells about the King's promise of the Prince of Peace, who would save humankind from sin; the Living Word fulfilled those promises when the Prince of Peace came to earth and suffered and died on a cross.

The Living Word is the *fine flour* that will satisfy your hunger and nourish you spiritually. You have been created with this spiritual hunger so that you will stay in direct communication with the King and receive you sustenance from Him. For this reason, your very life depends on being fed spiritually! The King's Word says that "He humbled you, causing you to hunger and then feeding you with manna. . . . to teach you that man does not live on bread alone but on every word that comes from the mouth of the LORD" (Deuteronomy 8:3). The King wants you to come to His banquet table and feast upon the Word, for you are a partaker of Christ and share in His life.

To "feast" means not to just eat but also "to take pleasure and delight" in eating.[1] In other words, the King wants you to not only read the Bible but also take pleasure and delight in the Word by memorizing it and hiding it in your heart. As you do, you will discover a sweetness that comes from spending time in the King's presence. This is the *honey* in your special diet. Listen once again to the Word:

> The law of the LORD is perfect. . . . The statutes of the LORD are trustworthy. . . . The precepts of the LORD are right. . . . The commands of the LORD are radiant. . . . They are sweeter than honey, than honey from the comb.
>
> —Psalm 19:7-8,10b

As you feast on the King's Word daily, you will begin to savor the sweetness of the King's love. This will nourish your innermost being—the secret place deep within your heart—and cause you to possess a gentle and quiet spirit. As others notice this unfading beauty within you, they will begin to recognize the fruit of the Spirit that Paul describes in Galatians 5:22-23: "Love, joy, peace, patience, kindness, goodness, faithfulness, gentleness and self-control." The King's Word will become real in your life as you join with Paul and proclaim, "For in my inner being I delight in God's law" (Romans 7:22). You will be a partaker of the King's divine nature.

This is why it is of utmost importance for you to not only feast on the Word but also *savor* every morsel. To "savor" means to take great delight in something, and as you savor the King's Word, it will cause you to deeply reflect upon it. This will enable you to be fruitful in your spiritual life, which is pleasing to the King. Consider what the scribe David wrote:

> [The King's Word is] sweeter than honey, than honey from the comb. . . . May the words of my mouth and the meditation of my heart be pleasing in your sight, O LORD.
> —Psalm 19:10b,14a

When you savor and meditate on the Word, it will be pleasing in the King's sight. You will bring glory to the King and will be ready to use the sword of the Spirit. You will be prepared to move forward in battle and fend off the enemy's attacks. As the psalmist wrote:

> Oh, how I love your law! I meditate on it all day long.... I have kept my feet from every evil path so that I might obey your word. I have not departed from your laws, for you yourself have taught me. How sweet are your words to my taste, sweeter than honey to my mouth.
> —Psalm 119:97,101-103

This is when the sweetness and the gentleness of the King will begin to reveal itself deep within your inmost being, which will cause you to possess the unfading beauty of a gentle and quiet spirit. For as you feast upon His Word through memorization and savor it through meditation, it will keep your feet from every evil and allow you to walk the path of righteousness. As the King's Word says:

> Be careful to follow every command I am giving you today, so that you may live and increase and may enter and possess the land that the LORD promised on oath to your forefathers. Remember how the LORD your God led you all the way in the desert these forty years, to humble you and to test you in order to know what was in your heart, whether or not you would keep his commands. He humbled you, causing you to hunger and then feeding you with manna, which neither you nor your fathers had known, to teach you that man does not live on bread alone but on every word that comes from the mouth of the LORD. . . . Observe the commands of the LORD your God, walking in his ways and revering him. For the LORD your God is bringing you into a good land. . . . a land with wheat and barley, vines and fig trees, pomegranates, *olive oil and honey*; a land where bread will not be scarce and you will lack nothing. . . . When you have eaten and are satisfied, praise the LORD your God for the good land he has given you.
>
> —Deuteronomy 8:1-3,6-10, emphasis added

As you follow the King and walk in His ways, He will lead you to a good land flowing with *olive oil* and honey. It's interesting to note that "along with other staples, such as grain and wine, oil was seen as an essence of life and a tangible sign of God's blessing and favor."[2] As you partake of this diet that satisfies your spiritual hunger, you will not only walk in His ways and revere Him, but, better yet, you will also receive the King's blessing and favor. When you recognize this in your life, you will discover another reason why you were given life: to praise Him. For you are a partaker of a heavenly calling.

The King's special beauty treatment will not only nourish you spiritually but also protect your life. Never forget that Lucifer, the destroyer, is looking for those whom he can devour. He will do anything within his power to keep you from possessing the unfading beauty of a gentle and quiet spirit. However, when you partake of the King's special diet and receive spiritual nourishment from Him, it will keep you in direct contact with Him. This is vital, because in war, communication with the commander is of the utmost importance. Without communication, the battle will be lost.

The United States knew the importance of having constant communication on the front lines during World War II. For this reason, the military went to great lengths to develop a secret code that the enemy would not be able to crack. This code, based on the Navajo Indian language, "was vital [to the Americans'] victory at Saipan and every major battle in the Pacific."[3] It was never broken, and it was one of the reasons that the United States was ultimately able to win the war.[4] In the same way, the only way for you to survive and be victorious is by maintaining direct communication with the King, for He is also known as the Commander of the Lord's army. He desires to direct every step you take so you can have victory.

Note that direct communication involves *two-way* communication. You speak with the King through prayer, and the King responds to you through His Word. Like the Navajo language, the King's Word is the secret code through which He gives you your marching orders. As you read, memorize, meditate and apply it, the King is able to speak to you through His "still small voice" (1 Kings 19:12, NKJV). He may use a story you read to speak to you, or He may just use one or two words in a verse.

Many times in my walk with the King, He has used just a word or two to direct my steps. During one time of confusion, I heard Him say, "Be still" (Psalm 46:10). During a time of fear, I heard Him say, "Perfect peace" (Isaiah 26:3). During a time of weariness, I heard Him speak, "Complete the task" (Acts 20:24). Each word was like a secret code to my heart because I had taken the time to prepare for battle. The moment I heard His still small voice, the verse I had memorized and meditated upon immediately came to my mind, and I was able to apply it to my situation. The King directed my steps so I could praise Him with my life.

As you meditate on the King's Word, partake of the *fine flour* that is the Bread of Life and realize that you share in that life. Feast upon this truth as you declare, *"I am a partaker of Christ and share in His life."*

You are also a partaker of His divine nature. Savor the flavor and sweetness of this fact like *honey* as you reflect, *"I am a partaker of His divine nature."*

You are a partaker of a heavenly calling. Devour the thick, rich *oil* of this blessing and favor as you say, *"I am a partaker of a heavenly calling."*

You are able to walk in the King's way and in the path of righteousness, for you have direct communication with your Commander as He guides you through life. Although you are in the midst of a battlefield, He will supply all your needs because of His great love. With this in mind, praise Him, for this is one of the reasons why you were given life. Walk forward as you proclaim it: *"I am able to walk in His way!"*

Until I can write again, remember to feast upon His Word. Then the unfading beauty of a gentle and quiet spirit will shine forth from deep within for all to see.

Enjoying the bountiful feast,

Your Well-Fed Servant

Chapter Twenty One

Clothed in Prayer

You Are Able to Approach the King

*In him and through faith in him
we may approach God with freedom and confidence.*
Ephesians 3:12

*Let us then approach the throne of grace with confidence,
so that we may receive mercy and find grace
to help us in our time of need.*
Hebrews 4:16

$\mathscr{D}$ear Beloved Believer,

In my last letter, I explained the vital importance of maintaining good communication with the Commander on the battlefield, for without this two-way-communication, Lucifer, the destroyer, will have the upper hand in the battle. I also explained how the King communicates with you and how you can listen for His voice. Now it is time for you to learn how to effectively communicate *with Him*. Let's begin by looking one last time at what the apostle Paul wrote about the armor of God in the book of Ephesians:

> Finally, my brethren, be strong in the Lord and in the power of His might. Put on the whole armor of God, that you may be able to stand against the wiles of

[Lucifer,] the devil. For we do not wrestle against flesh and blood, but against principalities, against powers, against the rulers of the darkness of this age, [and] against spiritual hosts of wickedness in the heavenly places. Therefore take up the whole armor of God, that you may be able to withstand in the evil day, and having done all, to stand. . . . praying always with all prayer and supplication in the Spirit, being watchful to this end with all perseverance and supplication for all the saints.

—Ephesians 6:10-13,18, NKJV

When you examine this passage closely, you will see that prayer is the final piece of top-secret military equipment the King provides to you. Furthermore, like the other pieces, it must be equipped properly in order for it to function in your life the way the King intends. Paul lists exactly how you can do this: (1) pray always, (2) pray in the Spirit, (3) be watchful in prayer, (4) persevere in prayer, and (5) provide supplication for all the saints through prayer.

Let's look at the first principle: *pray always*. In the book of Matthew, we read one of the Prince's teachings on prayer. He said:

When you pray, do not be like the hypocrites, for they love to pray standing in the synagogues and on the street corners to be seen by men. I tell you the truth, they have received their reward in full. But when you pray, go into your room, close the door and pray to your Father, who is unseen. Then your Father, who sees what is done in secret, will reward you. And when you pray, do not keep on babbling like the pagans, for they think they will be heard because of their many words. Do not be like them, for your Father knows what you need before you ask him.

—Matthew 6:5-8

In this passage, the Prince of Peace states that you are not to use prayer for show or even to babble on and on, for the King knows what you need even before you ask. But this raises some important questions: If the King already knows what you need, why does Paul state that you must pray always? Why even pray at all?

Remember that the King desires to have an intimate relationship with you. He wants you to share every detail of your life with Him. As the scribe Jeremiah writes, speaking for the King Himself: "Then you will call upon me and come and pray to me, and I will listen to you. You will seek me and find me when you seek me with all your heart" (Jeremiah 29:12-13). If you truly desire to seek after the King with all of your heart, you need to "pray without ceasing . . . for this is the will of God in Christ Jesus for you" (1 Thessalonians 5:17-18, NKJV). This means that from the moment your eyes open in the morning, it is time to pray. I love what the psalmist wrote:

> In the morning, O LORD, you hear my voice; in the morning I lay my requests before you and wait in expectation.
>
> —Psalm 5:3

John Bunyan once stated, "He who runs from God in the morning will scarcely find Him the rest of the day."[1] If you can't take time to meet with the King at the start of your day, you won't have success in making time for Him during your day when things get the most hectic. So begin each day with prayer.

But how do you *pray without ceasing* throughout your day? The answer has to do with your idea of what prayer actually looks like. Note what Wiersbe says: "The prayer posture of closing the eyes, bowing the head, and folding the hands is not found in Scripture. The Jews prayed with their eyes open towards heaven and their hands lifted towards God."[2] Prayer is not an activity that is to only take place in the King's house or in other designated locations. Instead, the King wants His people's *hearts* to be in continual communication with Him. This is what it means to *pray without ceasing.*

As you go through your day, pray to the King using your "still small voice." This is the quiet voice you use to form your thoughts. Talk to Him about your difficulties. Talk to Him about decisions that must be made. Talk to Him about anything and everything. Remember that He desires a real, personal, intimate relationship with you. He desires to spend time with you. For this reason, you are able to approach Him with confidence. He loves you deeply. Never forget that!

Of course, this does not mean that you come before the King with a long list of wants and desires. He is not some genie at your beck and call. The King is God—Jehovah-Elyon, "the Lord Most High," and it is only because of *who you are in Christ* that you are even allowed into His presence. So instead, when you communicate with the King in prayer, pray according to His will. Listen once again to the Word:

> This is the confidence we have in approaching God: that if we ask anything *according to his will*, he will hear us.
>
> —1 John 5:14, emphasis added

As James notes, when you pray from selfish motives, "You do not receive, because you ask with wrong motives, that you may spend what you get on your pleasures" (James 4:3). So, when you go to the King in prayer, pray according to His will for your life. Never forget that the King knows the plans He has for you. In fact, as He declared through

His scribe Jeremiah, He has "plans to prosper you and not to harm you, plans to give you a hope and a future" (Jeremiah 29:11). Pray according to the King's will to prevent Lucifer, the traitor, from causing you to stumble and fall. It is only when you are in the King's perfect will that you will be able to stand firm in the thick of battle and be in constant communication with your Commander.

The second principle Paul notes in wielding the weapon of prayer is to *pray in the Spirit*. This simply means to be led by the Royal Counselor when you pray. As I wrote to you in a previous letter, it is through the power of the Royal Counselor that you are able to stand in the face of the enemy's attacks. Many times you will not even know what to pray in a given situation, and it is in these moments that you can rely on the Royal Counselor to lead you and guide you. Listen to what Paul says:

> Likewise the Spirit helps us in our weakness. For we do not know what to pray for as we ought, but the Spirit himself intercedes for us with groanings too deep for words. And he who searches hearts knows what is the mind of the Spirit, because the Spirit intercedes for the saints according to the will of God.
> — Romans 8:26-27, ESV

As Brian Brodersen writes, "There's nothing quite as wonderful or thrilling as being empowered by the Holy Spirit in prayer. The heart is impassioned. The mind is clear. Every thought is ordered. Praise, petitions, and intercessions flow freely. . . . Seek to pray in the Spirit. Spend time asking the Lord to lead before you begin your prayer time."[3] This action of praying in the Spirit will build your faith and enable you to walk in the Spirit. Listen once again to the King's Word:

But you, beloved, building yourselves up on your most
holy faith, praying in the Holy Spirit.

—Jude 1:20, NKJV

Oswald Sanders once wrote, "The very fact that God
lays a burden of prayer on our hearts and keeps us praying is
evidence that He purposes to grant the answer."[4] This should
be a great encouragement to you, for it means that you can
know that the King, in His perfect timing, will answer your
request. What is even more wonderful is that He allows you
to be a part of His master plan by praying in the Spirit.

The third principle Paul notes is to be *watchful in prayer.*
In Colossians 4:2, Paul writes, "Devote yourselves to prayer,
being watchful and thankful," and in Romans 12:12, he
states, "Be joyful in hope, patient in affliction, faithful in
prayer." You are to be alert and on guard, always ready to
do battle in prayer. So when you see the King working in
your life, go to Him in prayer. When you see the enemy
attacking, go to the King in prayer. If a fellow believer is
struggling, pray to the King for that person. Get a prayer
partner, for the Prince of Peace Himself has said, "Where
two or three come together in my name, there am I with
them" (Matthew 18:20).

The fourth principle is to *persevere in prayer.* This simply
means to not give up when you feel your prayers are not being
answered. It means trusting that the King *does* care and that
He *is* listening, even though He may seem silent. As the scribe
Peter states, "Cast all your anxiety on [the King] because he
cares for you" (1 Peter 5:7). Remember that one of the King's
names is Jehovah-Shamman, "the Lord Is Present." He is always with you, and He will never forget you.

In a previous letter, I told you how the prophet Daniel
once persevered in prayer when no answer came from the
King. Daniel had been given a vision concerning a com-

ing great war, and it caused him such distress that for three weeks he mourned, ate no choice foods, and prayed to the King. Yet he received no answer. Finally, a messenger from the King arrived, who said to Daniel, "Do not be afraid. . . . *Since the first day that you set your mind to gain understanding and to humble yourself before your God, your words were heard*, and I have come in response to them." (Daniel 10:12, emphasis added). The angel had been dispatched immediately, but the enemy had prevented him from reaching Daniel with the answer. At this point, Daniel understood that unanswered prayer often indicates the intensity of the spiritual battle that was taking place beyond his view.

Silence should encourage you to fight harder. Silence should inspire you to use your secret weapon of prayer to fight the battle in the spiritual realm. Silence should indicate that your faith in the King is being tested to develop perseverance. So push through and persevere until the answer comes. As Brodersen writes, "One of the greatest obstacles to perseverance in prayer is the same one faced by the apostles themselves. Jesus said of them, 'The spirit is willing, but the flesh is weak' (Matthew 26:41). To persevere in prayer takes commitment, discipline and self-sacrifice."[5]

The fifth and final principle is to *provide supplication for all the saints* through prayer. The word "supplication" simply means to make a humble request. So, when you come before the Lord your King, humbly lift up your fellow believers before His throne. Pray for your pastor, for your friends, for those who are serving as missionaries, and for those in the Kingdom who are sick and suffering. As Brodersen points out, "You can have a worldwide ministry and never leave your own city limits by making supplication for all the saints."[6] In fact, one of the things that touched my heart the deepest while serving as a missionary in Eastern Europe was to learn that people I didn't even know were praying for me. It showed me how much the King loved me—He had impressed my need for prayer upon a stranger's heart.

Perhaps one of the most effective ways to pray is to simply lift up the Word in your communication with the King. As Bond writes, "Prayer is generated by the Word of God, guided by the will of God, and given by the Spirit of God."[7] Prayer and the Word go hand in hand, for when you pray the Word, you allow the King to guide your prayers and empower you with His Spirit, the Royal Counselor.

George Mueller, perhaps best known for his steadfast faith, read the King's Word from cover to cover more than 200 times during his lifetime. Even more astounding, according to Bond, is that for 100 of those times, Mueller read through the Word while he was on his knees. Mueller had experienced the power of the King's Word, and He understood that powerful, effective prayer was guided by the King's will. When asked toward the end of his life why so many of his prayers had been answered, Mueller replied, "I've prayed according to the Word of God. I pray the promises. I put my finger on the promise and then pray it. Then I say to God, 'Here it is. You wrote it down. It's in writing, so I'm anticipating some wonderful activity here.'"[8]

Learn from the example of Daniel and George Mueller. These two mighty men of the faith did not pray out of their selfish fleshly desires, but instead used the King's Word to effectively wield the secret weapon of prayer. So sharpen your skills as a trained warrior of the King and use this powerful weapon to do damage to Lucifer and destroy his many schemes.

With all this in mind, remember that you are able to approach the King with confidence. Stand tall as you state it: *"I am able to approach the King with confidence."*

You are also able to walk according to the Spirit. Let Him hear you proclaim it: *"I am able to walk according to the Spirit."*

As you do, you can cast all your cares upon Him. Lift the load off your shoulders as you place it on His and say, *"I am casting all my cares upon Him."*

When you have removed the burden, you are able to persevere. Say it with renewed strength: *"I am able to persevere."*

Never forget that you are able to approach the King with freedom. Go forth boldly as you state it, *"I am able to approach the King with freedom."*

Always remember that you were given life to have an intimate relationship with the King. Until my next letter, know that you are being lifted up in prayer.

Standing in His presence,
Your Interceding Servant

Chapter Twenty Two

Perfect Beauty

You Are Chosen to Bear Fruit

You did not choose me, but I chose you
and appointed you to go and bear fruit—
fruit that will last.
John 15:16a

𝒟ear Beloved Believer,

It is with a bittersweet heart that I write this letter to you. Bitter, for this is the last letter that I will send; but sweet, because I know that you are now fully prepared to serve the King. Throughout my letters, I have attempted to show you who you are in Christ, the King's Son, the Prince of Peace. In this closing letter, I want to encourage you to always look at who you are in Him and not at what someone may say, or even what you yourself may think. Never forget that *you are loved deeply*. You are not a mistake, for the King Himself wove you together in your mother's womb.

Also remember that you were created in the King's own image, that He chose you to be His own, and that He has set you apart for His service. The King has amazing plans for you, and He has called you to do a great work. This is yet another reason why you were given life—and it holds the key to the King's perfect will, His divine purpose, for your time on this earth. Grasping hold of this key will cause your life to have true meaning and fulfillment. Look at the final verse of the passage we have been reading in the book of Ezekiel:

> Your fame spread among the nations on account of your beauty, because the splendor I had given you made your beauty perfect, declares the Sovereign LORD.
>
> —Ezekiel 16:14

The King bestows this perfect beauty upon you so your life will have meaning and fulfillment as you reflect His splendor to those around you. You are the light of the world (see Matthew 5:14), so allow the radiance of the Prince of Peace to shine from your life so others will see the King's glory and be drawn to Him. The King has plans for you—plans to prosper you and not to harm you (see Jeremiah 29:11)—and the work He has set before you may be as far-reaching as to impact other nations.

As Paul wrote, you are "God's workmanship, created in Christ Jesus to do good works, which God prepared in advance for us to do" (Ephesians 2:10). The King has created you in Christ Jesus, the Prince of Peace, to do these works for Him. As you follow His will for your life, you glorify Him to all who are watching.

You are the King's co-worker. The Prince of Peace has appointed you to go and bear fruit—fruit that will last. As a matter of fact, you are called to testify about Him:

> So do not be ashamed to testify about our Lord, or ashamed of me [Paul] his prisoner. But join with me in suffering for the gospel, by the power of God, who has saved us and called us to a holy life—not because of anything we have done but because of his own purpose and grace.
>
> —2 Timothy 1:8-9

Remember that it is not about you but about the King of kings, the Prince of Peace, and the Royal Counselor—the one and only living God revealed in three persons. The King desires you to find your identity *only* in Christ and in what He has done for you to pay the price for your salvation. In view of this wonderful truth, I pray that these words from Paul become a way of life for you:

> Therefore, I urge you, brothers, in view of God's mercy, to offer your bodies as living sacrifices, holy and pleasing to God—this is your spiritual act of worship. Do not conform any longer to the pattern of this world, but be transformed by the renewing of your mind. Then you will be able to test and approve what God's will is—his good, pleasing and perfect will.
>
> — Romans 12:1-2

This is the King's perfect will for your life: to offer yourself as a living sacrifice so you will bear fruit. This is your spiritual act of worship to Him. Do not conform any longer to the pattern of this world—and all that the world believes is good and beautiful—but be transformed by the renewing of your mind. For when you break away from the world's mindset and allow the King to transform you, you will be able to test and approve what the King's will is for your life—His good, pleasing and perfect will. You will reflect the King's perfect beauty and be a light to others in a dark world.

As I have said throughout my letters, you were created to have intimate fellowship with the King. You were created to praise Him, to glorify Him, to be His witness and to reflect His glory. When you offer yourself as a living sacrifice and allow the King to use you, He will make you into an ambassador for the Prince of Peace, "as though God were making his appeal through [you]" (2 Corinthians 5:20a). As you dedicate your life to *serving* Him with your whole heart, He will reveal His will to you and show you the course He wishes you to follow.

Now, if you have never before served the King in this way, there are many ways for you to begin. First, take the time to find out what ministry and volunteer work is available in your community or in your church. There are usually many opportunities for volunteer work in hospitals, retirement homes, crisis pregnancy centers, shelters for abused women, shelters for the homeless, and even with children at parks and recreation centers. There are also many needs within a church, from children's ministry to seniors' ministry, that you could help fulfill. Get on the Internet and research the needs that are available, and then take time to pray and ask the King in which ministries He wants you to be involved. As you serve Him you will walk in His Great Light, the one and only true light, the Light of the World.

Make a time commitment of six months or so and pledge to serve the King with your whole heart and to the best of your ability. If you find that this is not the work for you after serving for several months, that's fine—just move on to the next opportunity. But don't stop serving Him! If you find that you are not sure of where to serve next, research the needs again and repeat the process. Remember that the King will use all kinds of situations to mold you into the person He wants you to become. So stick to the commitment you made and let your life bring glory and honor to the King.

In my early years of serving the King, I wanted to work with teenagers, but there was not an opening for me to do this. So I started serving in the children's ministry with the two-year-olds. The King used this time to prepare me for His divine purpose, and then He moved me as a teacher into the kindergartener room. That was scary for me, because for the first time I was instructing five-year-olds, but that is where I learned to teach. Soon He moved me to working with the teen girls—what fun! In time, He took me further still, beyond my imagination, and soon He had me directing the children's ministry and teaching adults how to be teachers. All this was in the King's plan for me, because He was using every position to direct me to His perfect will for my life, which, interestingly enough, had nothing to do with children but had everything to do with teaching.

During all this time, the King was implanting deep within my heart His vision and divine purpose for my life. Soon He impressed upon me the desire to begin a discipleship ministry for women and teenagers that would help them restore their broken hearts so they could be all that the King created them to be. Just as this ministry was beginning, I was asked to go on a short-term missions trip to Bulgaria to teach people how to be Sunday School teachers. Once there, the King miraculously opened the door for me to teach about abortion and its terrible aftermath. He used every job to train me for His divine purpose so my life could bring glory and honor to Him, the One and Only who deserves all the glory.

I share this example to encourage you to step out in faith and serve the King in any work He puts on your heart. No task is too small or insignificant in the Kingdom. In fact, the Prince of Peace has said that He who is faithful with the little things will be given more (see Matthew 25:23). And Paul wrote, "Whatever you do, work at it with all your heart, as working for the Lord, not for men, since you know that you will receive an inheritance from the Lord as a reward. It is the Lord Christ you are serving" (Colossians 3:23-24).

There is one final word of warning that I must give you so that Lucifer, the betrayer, will not cause you to stumble and fall. Throughout these letters, we have been studying Ezekiel 16:4-14, which, as I have mentioned, is an allegory about the unfaithfulness of the Israelites but is also an allegory for our lives in Christ. In this passage, Ezekiel refers to the Israelites (and us) as "the bride," and he describes all the King did for her. However, Ezekiel then goes on to tell us that the bride fell into terrible sins, most of which stemmed from the sin of self and pride:

> But you trusted in your beauty and used your fame to become a prostitute. You lavished your favors on anyone who passed by and your beauty became his. You took some of your garments to make gaudy high places, where you carried on your prostitution. Such things should not happen, nor should they ever occur. You also took the fine jewelry I gave you, the jewelry made of my gold and silver, and you made for yourself male idols and engaged in prostitution with them. And you took your embroidered clothes to put on them, and you offered my oil and incense before them. Also the food I provided for you—the fine flour, olive oil and honey I gave you to eat—you offered as fragrant incense before them. That is what happened, declares the Sovereign LORD.
>
> —Ezekiel 16:15-19

Beware! Lucifer, the schemer, will try to use these same sins to lead you down the path of self-destruction. Never forget that the King loves you so deeply that He gives you a choice—the choice to follow Him and the plans He has for you, or the choice to follow your own fleshly desires. Be warned that if you follow your own fleshly desires, it eventually will lead to the sin of pride.

Pride is especially dangerous because it can creep in unawares and destroy any ministry the King gives to you. So be prepared. If someone tells you that you are wonderful because of what the King is doing in your life, reflect all the glory to Him, for He is the one who truly deserves all the praise. Don't forget that it is all about Him and not about you. Otherwise, John's words in Revelation 18:14-17a may come true in your life: "The fruit you longed for is gone from you. All your riches and splendor have vanished, never to be recovered. . . . Woe! Woe, O great city, dressed in fine linen, purple and scarlet, and glittering with gold, precious stones and pearls! In one hour such great wealth has been brought to ruin!" What a shame! Don't allow this to happen in your life. Instead, die to self and live for Christ, the Prince of Peace, so that your life will bear fruit that will last.

Never forget that the King has given you His armor to equip you to stand firm, and you adorn the breastplate of righteousness every time you move the truth of who you are in Christ from your head to your heart. For this reason, grasp hold of who you are in Christ! For you are the light of the world. Shine brightly as you say, *"I am the light of the world."*

In view of this truth, walk in the Light so you can walk in the King's perfect will and His divine purpose. Radiantly walk forward as you gloriously proclaim, *"I am able to walk in the Light!"*

Remember that you were created to do good works. Let Him hear you rejoice in the labor as you say, *"I am created to do good works."*

You are the King's coworker. Declare it: *"I am the King's coworker."*

You are appointed to go and bear fruit. Delight in it as you anticipate the harvest: *"I am appointed to go and bear fruit."*

You are called by the King to testify about Him. Announce it for all to hear: *"I am called by the King to testify about Him."*

Yet not only that, but you are also called to serve the King. Offer yourself as you humbly proclaim, *"I am called to serve the King."*

In fact, you are called to offer yourself as a living sacrifice. As you determine in your heart to lay down your life for the King and set aside your own desires, sacrificially say, *"I am called to offer myself as a living sacrifice."*

And don't forget that you are an ambassador for the Prince of Peace. Stand tall and regal as you declare, *"I am His ambassador."*

This is the reason why you were given life! In view of this marvelous truth, allow the King to give your life true meaning and fulfillment as you die to self and live for Christ each day. Remember your Prince's last words before He ascended to heaven, for they represents your *Great Commission* on this earth:

> All authority in heaven and on earth has been given to me. Go therefore and make disciples of all nations, baptizing them in the name of the Father and of the Son and of the Holy Spirit, teaching them to observe all that I have commanded you. And behold, I am with you always, to the end of the age.
> —Matthew 28:18-20, ESV

Enjoying the Great Commission,
Your Servant Whose Life Has True Meaning

About the Author

In 1988, Cherie rededicated her life to the Lord, and soon after God began performing His gentle surgery deep within her heart to heal her of her deep heart hurts. After leading her through a process of recovery, God began impressing on her that she needed to help others with similar hurts and show them how to apply His Word to their lives. In 1993, she co-founded Strong-ARM (Abortion Recovery Ministry) to help women deal with issues of abortion and began teaching purity seminars to help teens make wiser choices. When women started to attend her workshops for issues other than abortion, she changed the name to the Truth and Hope Ministry to better encompass the scope of the work.

In 1999, Cherie wrote her first book titled *Go in Peace!* to help women deal with post-abortion issues. When she was unable to find a curriculum for her workshop that was 100 percent biblically based, she began writing the *Go in Peace! Leader's Manual* and *Go in Peace! Student Workbook*. This curriculum was written for individuals attending her seminars who were suffering from any deep heart hurt issues—such as rejection, rape, abortion and abuse, to name just a few.

In 2001, Cherie and her husband, Keith, opened the non-profit Truth and Hope Foundation in Sofia, Bulgaria, to help women and teens heal from their deep heart hurts. In 2006, she joined the staff of Calvary Chapel Murrieta, where she is the overseer and trainer of the women's biblical counseling ministry. In 2011 she also became the overseer of the women's discipleship ministry at Calvary Chapel of the Harbour. Today, in addition to writing, Cherie loves to travel and teach God's Word and can often be found teaching various topics at women's retreats and teen's seminars. Cherie has two daughters, who are both married to godly young men, and a growing number of grandchildren.

The sale of this book helps to further Cherie and her family's ministry work in the United States, Eastern Europe and wherever God sends them.

For more information about Cherie or her books, or if you would like to invite her to teach at one of your events, visit:

www.cheriefresonke.com
www.sunflowerpress.net

Don't forget to visit her blog while on her webpage. She usually posts a new blog weekly to encourage her readers. You can also subscribe to this by clicking on the "subscribe to feed" button.

For more information about the Truth and Hope Foundation in Sofia, Bulgaria, visit:

www.truthandhope.net

If you want to know what Cherie is up to, follow her on Facebook or Twitter at:

www.facebook.com/cherie.fresonke
www.twitter.com/CherieFresonke

To order additional copies of this title, the companion Bible study or any of the other books she has written (quantity discounts are available), visit our website at:

www.sunflowerpress.net

Or write to:

Sunflower Press
P.O. Box 813
Seal Beach, CA 90740

Endnotes

Chapter 2: Woven Together

1. *Holman Bible Dictionary.* "Image of God," on CD-ROM, (Quick Verse 6.0. Hiawatha, IA: Parsons Technology, 1999).

Chapter 3: Wrapped in the Cord of Sin

1. Part of the preceding paragraph was adapted from *The New Me* discipleship curriculum (San Bernardino, CA: Pacific Youth Correctional Ministries, 2003), p. 31.

Chapter 4: Clothed in Garments of Salvation

1. *The NIV Study Bible* (Grand Rapids, MI: Zondervan, 1985), study notes p. 1442.
2. *The NIV Study Bible*, p. 1441.
3. *Strong's Exhaustive Concordance of the Bible* (Peabody, MA: Hendrickson Publishers), s.v. "sin," Strong's Greek # 264.
4. Nathan Ausubel, *The Book of Jewish Knowledge* (New York, NY: Crown Publishers, 1964), p. 259.

Chapter 5: Clothed in Fine Linen

1. Jon Courson, *The Gospel According to Matthew*, vol. II (Jacksonville, OR: Olive Press, 1997), p. 110.
2. *Strong's Exhaustive Concordance of the Bible* (Peabody, MA: Hendrickson Publishers), s.v. *tetelestai*, Greek # 5055.
3. Warren W. Wiersbe, *The Cross of Jesus* (Grand Rapids, MA: Baker Books, 1997), p. 109.

Chapter 6: Clothed in Wisdom

1. Warren W. Wiersbe, *The Strategy of Satan* (Wheaton, IL: Tyndale House, 1979), p. 11.
2. *The NIV Study Bible* (Grand Rapids, MI: Zondervan, 1985), study notes on Revelation 12:10.
3. *The NIV Study Bible*, study notes on Revelation 2:10.
4. *Holman Bible Dictionary.* Quick Verse 6.0 (Hiawatha, IA: Parsons Technology, 1999), s.v. "Satan," on CD-ROM.
5. Warren W. Wiersbe, *Be Rich* (Colorado Springs, CO: Chariot Victor Publishing, 1998), p. 164.
6. Ralph Earle, quoted in *Word Meanings in the New Testament* (Peabody, MA: Hendrickson Publishers, Inc. 1986), p. 296.
7. *The NIV Study Bible*, study note on Daniel 10:13 (see also Daniel 12:1).
8. *Strong's Exhaustive Concordance of the Bible* (Peabody, MA: Hendrickson Publishers), s.v. "powers," Greek #1849.
9. Ibid., s.v. "touch," Greek #680.
10. Earle, quoted in *Word Meanings in the New Testament*, p. 327.
11. Dr. Helen Kaplan, "How AIDS Is Transmitted Through Sex," *The Real Truth About Women and AIDS*, pp. 78-86.
12. Warren W. Wiersbe, *The Strategy of Satan* (Wheaton, IL: Tyndale House, 1979), p. 11.

Chapter 7: Clothed with Power

1. Chuck Smith, *Living Water* (Eugene, OR: Harvest House Publishers, 1996), p. 13.
2. Ibid., p. 7.
3. Ibid., p. 13.
4. *Strong's Exhaustive Concordance of the Bible* (Peabody, MA: Hendrickson Publishers), s.v. *para*, Greek # 3844.
5. Smith, *Living Water*, p. 82.
6. *Webster's Ninth New Collegiate Dictionary* (Springfield, MA: Merriam-Webster, 1988), s.v. "reveal."
7. *Webster's Ninth New Collegiate Dictionary*, s.v. "conviction."

8. Smith, *Living Water*, p. 38.
9. *Strong's Exhaustive Concordance of the Bible*, s.v. *epi*, Greek #1909.
10. Henry Gainey, *The Afterglow* (Costa Mesa, CA: The Word for Today, 1998), p. 27.
11. Smith, *Living Water*, pp. 276-277.
12. Gainey, *The Afterglow*, p. 32.
13. Chuck Smith, *Charisma Versus Charismania* (Costa Mesa, CA: The Word for Today, 1992), p. 32.

Chapter 8: Girded with the Belt of Truth

1. *Webster's Ninth New Collegiate Dictionary*, (Springfield, MA: Merriam-Webster, 1988), s.v. "gird."
2. Sylvia Charles, *Women in the Bible: Examples to Live By* (Tulsa, OK: Virgil Hensley Publishing, 1988), p. 1.
3. *Webster's Ninth New Collegiate Dictionary*, (Springfield, MA: Merriam-Webster, 1988), s.v. "integrity."

Chapter 9: Wearing the Most Beautiful of Jewels

1. *Webster's Ninth New Collegiate Dictionary* (Springfield, MA: Merriam-Webster, 1988), s.v. "righteousness."
2. Jon Courson, *The Gospel According to John*, vol. III (Jacksonville, OR: Olive Press, 1997), p. 121.
3. Bob Hoekstra, "The Exaltation of Self," lecture on cassette tape (Murrieta, CA: Living in Christ Ministries).

Chapter 10: Adorned in the Breastplate of Righteousness

1. Warren W. Wiersbe, *What to Wear to the War* (Lincoln, NE: Back to the Bible, 1986), p. 36.
2. *Holman Bible Dictionary*, "Arms and Armor," Quick Verse 6.0 computer software (Hiawatha, IA: Parsons Technology, Inc., 1999).
3. *Webster's Ninth New Collegiate Dictionary* (Springfield, MA: Merriam-Webster, 1988), s.v. "punishment."
4. *Webster's Ninth New Collegiate Dictionary*, s.v. "discipline."

Chapter 11: Covered by the King's Garment

1. Warren W. Wiersbe, *Be Committed* (Colorado Springs, CO: Chariot Victor Publishing, 1993), pp. 32-33.
2. *The NIV Study Bible* (Grand Rapids, MI: Zondervan, 1985), study notes on Ruth 3:4.
3. Ibid., study notes on Ruth 3:9.
4. *Webster's Ninth New Collegiate Dictionary* (Springfield, MA: Merriam-Webster, 1988), s.v. "redeemed."
5. Nathan Ausubel, *The Book of Jewish Knowledge* (New York: Crown Publishers, 1964), p. 259.
6. Jon Courson, *Tree of Life Bible Commentary: Ruth* (Jacksonville, OR: Applegate Christian Fellowship, 1997), p. 49.

Chapter 12: Free from Filthy Rags

1. *The NIV Study Bible* (Grand Rapids, MI: Zondervan, 1985), study notes on Ezekiel 16:9.
2. Janet Miteva, *Nessebur: A Town with a History* (Bulgaria: Format S, 2001), p. 15.
3. *Webster's Twenty-first Century Dictionary* (Nashville, TN: Thomas Nelson Publishers, 1993), s.v. "hoard."
4. *Webster's Ninth New Collegiate Dictionary* (Springfield, MA: Merriam-Webster, 1988), s.v. "hoard."
5. Ibid., s.v. "stuff."
6. *Webster's Twenty-first Century Dictionary*, s.v. "relic."
7. *Webster's Ninth New Collegiate Dictionary*, s.v. "treasure."
8. *The NIV Study Bible*, study notes on Isaiah 64:6.

Chapter 13: Adorned in the Leather Sandals of Peace

1. *Collins Paperback Dictionary and Thesaurus* (New York: Harper Collins Reference, 2006), s.v. "peace."
2. "Dictionary and Word Search for *Hetoimasia* (Strong's Greek #2091)," *Blue Letter Bible*, 2011. http://www.blueletterbible.org/lang/lexicon/lexicon.cfm? Strongs=G2091&t=NKJV. See also "Dictionary and Word Search for *Hetoimaz* (Strong's Greek #2090), Blue Letter Bible, 2011.

http:// www.blueletterbible.org/lang/lexicon/Lexicon.
cfm? Strongs=G2090&t=NKJV.

3. Danny Bond, *Clothed to Conquer* (Laguna Hills, CA: The
   Word Transfer, 1999), p. 43.
4. *Webster's Twenty-first Century Dictionary* (Nashville, TN:
   Thomas Nelson Publishers, 1993), s.v. "balance."

Chapter 14: Wearing Costly Garments

1. *The NIV Study Bible* (Grand Rapids, MI: Zondervan, 1985),
   study note on Isaiah 64:6.
2. Warren W. Wiersbe, *The Cross of Jesus* (Grand Rapids, MI:
   Baker Books, 1997), p. 32.
3. Jon Courson, *The Gospel According to John*, vol. III (Jacksonville, OR: Olive Press, 1997), p. 93.
4. Courson, *Jon Courson's Application Commentary New Testament* (Nashville, TN: Thomas Nelson, 2004), p. 582.
5. *The NIV Study Bible*, study notes on John 18:6.
6. Courson, *The Gospel According to Matthew*, vol. II (Jacksonville, OR: Olive Press, 1997), p. 121.
7. Henry Halley, *Halley's Bible Handbook* (Grand Rapids, MI:
   Zondervan, 1980), p. 549.
8. Wiersbe, *The Cross of Jesus*, p. 54.
9. *Strong's Exhaustive Concordance of the Bible* (Peabody, MA:
   Hendrickson Publishers, 2009), Greek #5218.
10. *Webster's Ninth New Collegiate Dictionary* (Springfield, MA:
    Merriam-Webster, 1988), s.v. "submission."
11. *Webster's Twenty-first Century Dictionary* (Nashville, TN:
    Thomas Nelson Publishers, 1993), s.v. "comply."
12. Wiersbe, *The Cross of Jesus*, p. 53.

Chapter 15: Equipped with the Shield of Faith

1. Danny Bond, *Clothed to Conquer* (Laguna Hills, CA: The
   Word Transfer, 1999). p. 67.

Chapter 16: Crowned with the Helmet of Victory

1. Warren Wiersbe, *Be Wise* (Colorado Springs, CO: Chariot
   Victor Publishing, 1983), p. 38.

Chapter 17: Crowned in Holiness

1. Warren Wiersbe, *Be Rich* (Colorado Springs, CO: Chariot Victor Publishing, 1998) p. 13-14.
2. Ibid., pp. 9-10.
3. Ibid., p. 10.
4. *Webster's Ninth New Collegiate Dictionary* (Springfield, MA: Merriam-Webster, 1988), s.v. "saint."
5. Ibid., s.v. "sanctity."
6. *Dictionary of Biblical Imagery* (Downers Grove, IL: Inter-Varsity Press, 1998), s.v. "sanctification."
7. *Blue Letter Bible*, s.v. "holiness," Strong's Hebrew #06944, dictionary and word search for qodesh. http://www.blueletterbible.org/lang/lexicon/lexicon. cfm?Strongs=H06944&t=KJV.
8. Ibid., s.v. "way," *Strong's* Hebrew #01870, dictionary and word search for derek. http://www.blueletterbible.org/lang/ lexicon/lexicon.cfm?Strongs=H01870&t=KJV.
9. *Blue Letter Bible* CD-ROM, Matthew Henry Commentary on Isaiah 35.
10. "Historic Royal Speeches and Writings Victoria (r. 1837–1901)," The British Monarchy website, November 11, 2007. http://www.royal.gov.uk/files/pdf.victoria.pdf.
11. *Quick Verse* CD-ROM, version 6.0 (The Learning Company, 1999), s.v. "crown."

Chapter 18: Adorned with Gold and Silver

1. *Blue Letter Bible* CD-ROM, version 1.0. David Guzik Study Guide for 1 Peter 1:3-5.
2. Warren Wiersbe, *Be Encouraged* (Colorado Springs, CO: Chariot Victor Publishing, 1994), p. 136.
3. Ibid., p. 137.

Chapter 19: Equipped with the Sword of the Spirit

1. Danny Bond, *Clothed to Conquer* (Laguna Hills, CA: The Word Transfer, 1999), p. 101.

2.   Ibid., p. 102.
3.   Ibid., p. 110.

Chapter 20: Clothed in Unfading Beauty

1.   *Webster's Ninth New Collegiate Dictionary* (Springfield, MA: Merriam-Webster, 1988), s.v. "feast."
2.   *Dictionary of Biblical Imagery* (Downers Grove, IL: Inter-Varsity Press, 1998), p. 603.
3.   John Woo, director, *Windtalkers* (Los Angeles, CA: MGM, 2002).
4.   Ibid.

Chapter 21: Clothed in Prayer

1.   John Bunyan, cited in Danny Bond, *Clothed to Conquer* (Laguna Hills, CA: The Word Transfer, 1999), p. 119.
2.   Warren Wiersbe, *The Strategy of Satan* (Wheaton, IL: Tyndale House, 1979). p. 139.
3.   Brian Brodersen, *Spiritual Warfare* (Costa Mesa, CA: The Word for Today, 1995). p. 64.
4.   Ibid., p. 64.
5.   Ibid., p. 66.
6.   Ibid., p. 67.
7.   Bond, *Clothed to Conquer*, p. 125.
8.   George Mueller, cited in Bond, *Clothed to Conquer*, p. 126.

Clothed in Righteousness— Bible Study

Cherie Fresonke

Did you enjoy *Clothed in Righteousness*?

If so, don't miss out on going deeper in your relationship with the King of kings. Order the companion *Clothed in Righteousness— Bible Study* today!

As you partake of each lesson you will have the resources to become all that God created you to be, and best yet, you will discover the reason why He gave you life.

This study is excellent for personal study, or as a group Bible study for women's ministries and home groups. Cherie is also available to teach at women's retreats and seminars just contact us today at www.sunflowerpress.net.

Available in stores and online!

Sunflowerpress.net

Go in Peace! Biblical Discipleship Curriculum
Cherie Fresonke

Do you know someone struggling with depression, anxiety, fear, rage, relationship difficulties and/or self-destructive behaviors such as alcohol and drug abuse, eating disorders, self-harm or even suicidal thoughts?

Do you desire to help but don't know how? This curriculum will give you the answer.

Depression, anxiety, outbursts of anger are just a few of the consequences associated with deep heart hurts. Cherie Fresonke uses the story of the Sinful Woman in Luke chapter 7 as the foundation to help heal the brokenhearted in this powerful, life-changing curriculum. This Bible study teaches practical application of God's Word to help set the captives free. Those learning from the pages within will soon discover their fear replaced with strength, depression with joy, anxiety with faith, and rage with rest. Best yet, they will discover what it means to go in peace!

Don't miss out! If you, yourself, would like to go through this material with Cherie then order the ***DVD Disciple Me!*** curriculum by visiting www.sunflowerpress.net or www.cheriefresonke.com today!

The *Go in Peace! Leader's Manual, Student Workbook* and book are available through our website at www.sunflowerpress.net as well as available for order through most on-line retailers.

Go in Peace!
Cherie Fresonke

"About 40 Percent of American Women Have Had Abortions."

—Newsweek.com

With a statistic as high as this, it is likely that you have a friend or relative who has made this tragic choice. Perhaps you have seen this person struggle with depression, anxiety, nightmares, outbursts of anger, over-protectiveness, relationship difficulties and/ or self-destructive behaviors (such as anorexia, bulimia, harming self, drugs, alcohol or suicidal thoughts). You may have wanted to help your friend, but you didn't know what to do or say.

Go in Peace! will give you the answer. This resource, which is excellent for personal study and for those who desire to be used by God more powerfully in ministering to people in need, will show you practical ways to apply God's Word to the hurting person's life so that she can be set free from the guilt, shame, hurt and pain associated with her decision. Although this book was written specifically for the issue of post-abortion, in reality it offers hope and healing for anyone who is hurting. It will show you how to be free from this pain so that you and your loved ones can *go in peace!*

Available in stores and online!

Sunflowerpress.net

Go in Peace for Teens

Cherie Fresonke

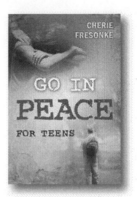

Do you know a teen struggling with depression? Anxiety? Rage? Drugs and alcohol? Cutting? Suicidal thoughts?

Ask anyone who works with teens and they'll tell you these problems have reached epidemic levels, and they cross all spectrums of our society—kids from all types of homes, living in all types of neighborhoods, attending all types of churches. Clearly, our teens need help and guidance to navigate the rough waters of current teen culture.

Cherie Fresonke's book, *Go in Peace for Teens*, helps teens identify the deep heart hurts driving these self-destructive behaviors and gives them tangible, step-by-step, life-changing help in learning how to give these hurts to God so He can heal them.

Go in Peace for Teens can be used as a workbook for personal study, or as a Bible study for pastors and counselors in one-on-one discipleship with teens. Parents looking for help in guiding their teens will also find this book useful.

Also available for any who would like to learn how to disciple hurting teenagers is the **Teen in Crisis DVD Curriculum.** You can order the curriculum by visiting www.sunflowerpress.net or www.cheriefresonke.com today!

The book *Go in Peace for Teens*
is available in stores and online!
Sunflowerpress.net